Sustainable Design Solutions from the Pacific Northwest

SUSTAINABLE DESIGN SOLUTIONS FROM THE PACIFIC NORTHWEST
Vikram Prakash, Series Editor

Architects of the Pacific Northwest have been celebrated for a long-standing respect for the environment and a holistic view of our place in it. This series spotlights innovative design achievements by contemporary Northwest architects whose work reinforces core principles and ethics of sustainable design. Reflecting cross-disciplinary inspirations ranging from environmental sciences to sociology and systems biology, the pioneering buildings and technologies profiled in this series share common aesthetic and social goals. Promoting maximum energy efficiency through extensive use of recycled materials and minimal dependence on mechanical systems for heat, ventilation, and waste management, these works demonstrate a profound and enduring love of the natural world and its ecological systems.

Studio at Large: Architecture in Service of Global Communities
by Sergio Palleroni, with Christina Eichbaum Merkelbach

Toward a New Regionalism: Environmental Architecture in the Pacific Northwest
by David E. Miller

TOWARD A NEW REGIONALISM

Environmental
Architecture in the
Pacific Northwest

TOWARD A NEW REGIONALISM

Environmental
Architecture in the
Pacific Northwest

David E. Miller

University of Washington Press
Seattle and London

Toward a New Regionalism is published with the assistance of grants from the University of Washington Architecture Publications Fund.

University of Washington Press
PO Box 50096, Seattle, WA 98145
www.washington.edu/uwpress

Library of Congress Cataloging-in-Publication Data

Miller, David E.
  Toward a new regionalism : environmental architecture in the Pacific Northwest /   David E. Miller.–1st ed.
      p. cm. – (Sustainable design solutions from the Pacific Northwest)
  Includes bibliographical references and index.
  ISBN 0-295-98494-5 (pbk. : alk. paper)
  1. Sustainable architecture–Northwest, Pacific. 2. Architecture–Environmental aspects–Northwest, Pacific. 3. Regionalism in architecture–Northwest, Pacific. I. Title. II. Series.
  NA2542.36.M55 2005
  720'.47'09795–dc22

The paper used in this publication meets the minimum requirements of American National Standard for Information Sciences—Permanence of Paper for Printed Library Materials, ANSI Z39.48-1984.

Design and composition by Christina Eichbaum Merkelbach

Frontmatter illustrations: (p. iv) Recycling portals with canopy, Vashon Island Transfer and Recycling Station, by Miller/Hull. Photo: Fred Housel. (p. viii) Windows wrap corners to gather light, Maple Valley Library, by Johnston Architects with Cutler Anderson Architects. Photo: Art Grice.

To Alix Henry and Susan Olmsted for their energetic assistance

CONTENTS

Preface and Acknowledgments   xi

Introduction: A New Regionalism   xv

1   CONDITIONS OF REGIONALISM   3
     The Pacific Northwest Region   3
     The Marine Coastal Climate   5
     The Northwest Style   5

2   SUSTAINABLE DESIGN IN THE PACIFIC NORTHWEST: A BRIEF HISTORY   11
     Northwest Coast Native Structures   13
     The Arts and Crafts Period   15
     Early Northwest Modernists   17
     The Northwest School   22
     The Northwest Contemporary Period: The 1970s   30
     The 1980s to the New Millennium   33

3   ENVIRONMENTAL STRATEGIES   35
     Earth   36
     Fire   41
     Air   46
     Water   47

4   SITE: BUILDING THROUGH ECOLOGICAL PLANNING   53
     Cedar River Watershed Education Center, King County, WA   55
     Vashon Island Transfer and Recycling Station, King County, WA   67
     Environmental Services Building, Pierce County, WA   73
     Maple Valley Library, Maple Valley, WA   79

5   LIGHT CONSTRUCTION: RESOURCE-CONSERVING BUILDING   85
     Bradner Garden Community Building, Seattle, WA   87
     Materials Testing Facility, Vancouver, BC   93
     Petite Maison de Weekend Revisited   99

6   LIGHT AND VENTILATION: CLIMATE-RESPONSIVE ENCLOSURE   103
     IslandWood, Bainbridge Island, WA   105
     Pier 56, Seattle, WA   111
     Telus/William Farrell Building Revitalization, Vancouver, BC   117

7   TECHNOLOGY AND MATERIALS: THE INTEGRATED FUTURE   123
     Seattle Justice Center and Seattle Civic Center Plan, Seattle, WA   125
     Bainbridge Island City Hall, Bainbridge Island, WA   131
     Jean Vollum Natural Capital Center, Pearl District, Portland, OR   137
     The Brewery Blocks, Pearl District, Portland, OR   141
     Wieden + Kennedy Building, Pearl District, Portland, OR   145

8   CONCLUSION   149

Appendix A. Glossary   153

Appendix B. Project Information   161

Notes and References   169

Index   172

PREFACE AND ACKNOWLEDGMENTS

The title of this book implies, on the one hand, a content concerned with green issues in the design of buildings. On the other hand, it suggests that there might be new directions emerging in architectural design—a holistic approach to creating buildings that comes from a regionally based, sustainable perspective. Thus, it is my intent in this book to explore the direct connection between concepts of sustainable design and the critical issues of regionalism and how together they should form the underpinnings for authentic and meaningful architectural form.

There are many regions around the world where the vernacular has been directly shaped by environmental responses, from the pueblos of the American Southwest to the stilt houses of Malaysia, and there are many examples of vernacular structures that are emulated today.

Interestingly, however, the Pacific Northwest lacks an enduring indigenous architecture. The coastal Native American longhouses that lined the shores of Puget Sound and the various sounds of British Columbia and southeastern Alaska were beautiful expressions of environmental conditions and sociocultural structure, but they did not form an indigenous Pacific Northwest architecture that has carried through to modern times.

This writer contends that not until the advent of the early Modernism produced by a post–World War II generation of architects did a Northwest Regional Style emerge. This regional style has continued to develop over the past fifty-plus years and, in various forms, has embraced elements of sustainable design. The sustainable features are not generally expounded when one reads the many manuscripts on Northwest Regionalism, but when one looks for the origins and development of modern environmentally conscious architecture, it is apparent that they lie in the essential principles of Modernism. As Christian Norberg-Schulz states in *Principles of Modern Architecture:*

> Regional character is an essential property of any authentic architecture. As all buildings form part of a concrete "here" they cannot be alike everywhere, but have to embody the particular qualities of a given place. From ancient times this quality has been recognized as the genius loci, and historical buildings normally had a distinct local flavor, although they often belonged to a general style. Architecture thus helped man to identify with the "spirit of the place," and offered him a sense of belonging and security.[1]

The core of sustainable design lies in responding to a "spirit of place." Architecture that heals the heart, our biological systems, and the environment is sustainable. It needs to be shaped by and for a region's conditions. The green past has relevance for the future.

(Opposite) The Pacific Northwest landscape. Decatur Island's forested slopes meet Lopez Sound. Photo: Miller/Hull

This book begins with a brief discussion of the environmental and cultural conditions of the Pacific Northwest region. Chapters 2 and 3 examine the attitudes and influences of important figures in the early Northwest Modern Movement and their seminal work with respect to environmentally conscious design. These chapters explore the principles of environmental architecture that work in the Pacific Northwest and which grow out of the specific climate and ecological factors. Chapters 4 through 7 are case studies that bring into focus current regional work in sustainable design by significant Pacific Northwest architects. The case studies are divided into four categories that represent future directions in planning and design: site, light construction, light and ventilation, and technology and materials. This work demonstrates how the ideas of a new regionalism and environmentally responsible design are intrinsically linked.

Through most of my career, I have enjoyed the challenges of integrating the practice of architecture with teaching. The ideas in this book grew through project development and research at The Miller/Hull Partnership, with professional peers doing groundbreaking work in sustainable design here in the Pacific Northwest, and through critical discussions with graduate students in the Department of Architecture at the University of Washington. I wish to acknowledge my cofounding partner, Robert Hull, for his contributions to the fields of energy conservation and environmental design over the past twenty-five years. Equally, I would like to acknowledge my students, who have asked the crucial questions about how one forms an architectural idea. In particular, Susan Olmsted's and Alix Henry's excellent research, case study documentation, and editorial comments have been invaluable. I also want to thank Vikram Prakash, Chair of the Department of Architecture at the University of Washington, for having the vision to initiate this book and to involve our publisher, the University of Washington Press, in the project. Finally, this book's content—the critical case studies—is the result of extraordinary work by Pacific Northwest architects who have created some of the best environmental design work in North America. They have supported the development of this book by collaborating on the text and contributing their materials for publication. Thank you, Peter Busby, Vancouver; John Patkau, Vancouver; Dave Goldberg, Mithun Architects + Designers + Planners, Seattle; Paul Olson and Nancy Rottle, Jones & Jones, Architects, Seattle; Sian Roberts and Scott Wolf, principals at The Miller/Hull Partnership, Seattle; Jim Cutler, Cutler Anderson Architects, Bainbridge Island, Washington; Scot Carr, SHED, Seattle; Jeff Stuhr, Holst Architects, Portland; and Brad Cloepfil, Allied Works Architecture, Portland.

Designing sustainable buildings can be one of the most important and challenging of architectural tasks. Yet many architects seem to experience a lack of motivation, a paralysis of will, to create powerful architectural solutions that blend the best of sustainable concepts with the poetic beauty of well-designed form. This resistance to embracing the values of sustainable design as significant contributing factors to shaping form is due in large part to the belief that sustainable architecture is a fashion, or a radical offshoot movement, and will not last. It is of vital importance to the discipline of architecture that we overturn this suspicion of environmental architecture—and we are running out of time. We should be looking at the pivotal relation between ecological values and the design of our physical environment.

(Opposite) Entry to the Environmental Services Building, Pierce County, Washington, by Miller/Hull. Scuppers deliver rainwater to detention ponds. Photo: Eckert & Eckert

INTRODUCTION:
A NEW REGIONALISM

For a greater part of the twentieth century and now into the twenty-first, architects have engaged in an ongoing debate on the apparent contradiction between the universal and the particular. The International Style, the most globally influential architectural movement since the Renaissance, promoted a universal approach. In opposition, Kenneth Frampton's 1982 essay on critical regionalism argued for an architecture that is conceived out of local conditions and resists being totally absorbed by the global imperatives of production and consumption. Despite Frampton's important treatise on architectural theory and the work of a few outstanding regional architects, there has been a continual melding of architectural style from one end of the globe to the other.

Fashion, however, is the enemy of integrity. Architects need to work toward a rational and timeless architecture that sustains the qualities of place. The imperative question then becomes, how does a designer determine the overall conception and realization of architectural form that captures the spirit and quality of place and at the same time addresses the compelling issue of our day—the world's ecological dysfunction?

Ecological dysfunction is signified by ozone depletion, air and water pollution, and global climate change caused by increasing human population and the resulting waste and pollution. Architecture is linked to this environmental degradation through resource extraction and transportation, offgassing of materials, consumption of electricity and other fuels for mechanical systems, and construction waste and wastewater. Failing to responsibly address these conditions impacts the entire earth, but the origins of the problems are fundamentally local. A designer must contend with these global concerns by connecting design to the spirit and natural conditions of a specific region.

As the architect Harwell Hamilton Harris states, "To be expressed, an idea must be built. To be built, it must be particularized, localized, set within a region."[1] This book seeks to illuminate those aspects of Northwest regionalism that have consistently supported an architecture aimed at environmental needs and priorities. All local cultures contain an essence that must be discovered or preserved and which expresses the uniqueness of a place. For architects in the Pacific Northwest, that essence is the fundamental understanding of the conditions of ecology and their effect on architectural values and meaning. Significant aspects of this essence lie in local geography, climate, and customs and involve the use and transformation of local, "natural" materials. While a truly responsible regionalism rejects the mimicking of vernacular forms, it embodies a causal relationship between the environment and architectural forms.

An environmental architecture provides for humanity's long-term needs, both physical and psychological, using only those resources the earth can

(Opposite) Reading room, with view of forest, at the Maple Valley Library, Maple Valley, Washington, by Johnston Architects with Cutler Anderson Architects. Photo: Art Grice

sustainably provide. Through modern engineering, architectural designers and their collaborating consultants have been able to produce reasonably comfortable conditions in almost any building in almost any climate. The engineering solutions associated with this architecture, however, have required high-grade energy in order to deal with the environmental conditions. Architects and engineers must reduce a building's reliance on the precious resources fueling these high-grade energy systems and yet still provide comfort for the occupants.

At the same time, essential elements and principles of sustainable design go beyond issues of energy conservation and material content. They must bring into play the qualities of space and form, flexibility for adaptive use over time, qualities of transparency and utilization of daylight, the free flow of air within a building, and fit with a particular site. There should be an aesthetic quality that both endures and heals the heart and ultimately renders a building worthy of preservation. These elements typically are contained in the work of Pacific Northwest regional designers, from the early work of the 1950s and 1960s modernists to the recent contemporary architecture of the new Northwest Regionalists.

Many journals and books that discuss Northwest Regionalism describe the structures as a wood-frame, post-and-beam style that engages its natural surroundings. Regional design in the Pacific Northwest goes well beyond these basic notions of a local architecture. This book investigates the inherent conditions that both expand and define the style known as Northwest Regionalism and have created the foundations for an architecture of sustainable-design principles.

First and foremost, every architect working in the Pacific Northwest has to acknowledge the unique conditions of the region's natural light— creatively, defensively, or provocatively. Northwest natural light is unique. The light of an overcast sky can be intense, and constant, but it differs greatly from direct sunlight. Hazy maritime cloud cover is common throughout the autumn, winter, and spring months and contrasts with the clear summer sky. Winter days are shorter than most others in the continental United States, and summer days are long, sunny, and bright. There is no single solution, no formula for the architectural response to light, but it is the singular condition that directly affects form and space. Designing for natural light opens possibilities for reducing energy through decreased use of artificial lighting, enhancing ventilation by natural methods, and engaging occupants with the natural rhythms of the day and the season.

Second, the dramatic landscape can play a mythic role. The Pacific Northwest architect can bow to a spectacular site and reflect it graciously, or abstract the environment with a provocative contrasting pose—both are legitimate and meaningful additions to the landscape. Since flat sites are virtually nonexistent in the western zones of the Pacific Northwest, topography is invariably a player in form-making. Whether a site is steep or gently sloped, the response is often to place the building on piers, which leads to a structure of post and beam that rests lightly on the land. This characteristic is generally associated with a Japanese influence; however, it is more a utilitarian and pragmatic reaction to topographic conditions. The frame of post and beam, which reduces material and is structurally very efficient, with applied siding, suspended panels, or glazed bays, is a contemporary architectural development credited to Seattle architects.

Last (although usually listed first), the Northwest Regional Style is characterized by its use of wood. Aside from being abundant, wood has offered Pacific Northwest architects infinite design opportunities. Its insulation value, structural capacity, versatility and adaptability for various construction conditions, and, ultimately, its natural beauty made it the material of choice. These elements of Northwest Regionalism, which characterized the early work of the modernist pioneers and to this day still define the Northwest Regional Style, are the basic building blocks of sustainable design.

More recently, the twenty-first century is bringing with it a transformation of design through advances in communication systems, digital design, and construction technology. Globally, this transformation has brought about a shift toward an expanding ecological consciousness in the design fields. The trend promises to be incredibly far-reaching, permeating all aspects of theory and practice for architects, landscape architects, planners, engineers, and builders.

These exciting directions within architectural design—the technological advances and focus on environmental sustainability—are manifested in the Pacific Northwest. With communications and technology companies in our own backyard and given our unique natural environment, architects in the Pacific Northwest, more than any other region in the world, have the opportunity to bring these elements together into a comprehensive design approach. Such an approach is much more about environmental-quality issues than about the form-making and material gymnastics prevalent in the obsessive and indulgent 1990s. Building is sustainable if it employs the most advanced technologies of the present and at the same time justifies their use in architectural solutions that meet not only the economic interests of the clients but also the aesthetic concerns of the architects, the changing needs of the users, and the ecological challenges facing humanity as a whole.

Welcome center at IslandWood, Bainbridge Island, Washington, by Mithun. Photo: Doug J. Scott/dougscott.com

Entry facade at the Pierce County Environmental Services Building, University Place, Washington. A featured case study sited on a former gravel quarry. Photo: Eckert & Eckert

Projects that integrate these factors have recently been completed or are currently being designed here in our region. These projects demonstrate important notions about sustainability, technology, and climate-generated form. Buildings become all the better when they are environmentally friendly. Architects should build upon these ideas and work toward a truly new and unique regional architecture.

THE CASE STUDIES

The projects featured as case studies in chapters 4–7 represent some of the most notable examples of Pacific Northwest architecture that incorporates sustainable design. Each project is considered in terms of its programmatic and conceptual framework with regard to its site and the opportunities presented by available resources. As in the prior discussion of natural conditions in the Pacific Northwest, the basic elements of earth, fire, air, and water provide the overall organization and the platform for comparison. Though many of the projects deal with similar conditions, each design response is remarkably different, underscoring the inherent variability in site- and climate-responsive architecture.

Each case study concludes with a brief discussion of some of the successes and shortcomings of the featured project with the intent of developing critical knowledge about sustainable architecture. Sustainable design holds tremendous opportunities, but, as with any practice of design, every decision carries a trade-off. The architect's challenge is to understand the trade-offs and make the best choices available within the given constraints. As we share our successes and shortcomings, and learn from one another, we will move toward a truly sustainable body of architecture that is solidly based in the Pacific Northwest.

These projects represent the state of sustainable design thinking at the time this book was written. Many Pacific Northwest projects currently in design or under construction contain strong concepts in sustainable design and would have been great additions to this manuscript. As with architecture, however, a book must meet its schedule and stay within its budget, and difficult choices had to be made. It's my hope that the notable projects not included here will find their way into future works by other authors.

The beautiful buildings recently completed and being designed in our region evoke the euphoric power of the Pacific Northwest's early modernist architecture. Our designers share this spirit. The region's architects are inspired, full of confidence and technical know-how, and committed to a constantly improving future.

TOWARD A NEW REGIONALISM

CHAPTER 1
CONDITIONS OF REGIONALISM

Many architectural writers and historians have documented the various elements generally regarded as characteristics that define Northwest Regionalism. In order to understand the elements that make up regional architecture, we must look at what the environment and culture have made possible or allowed. We need to examine the climate; the ecology, which includes soil, topography, and native flora; the technology of construction; and the stylistic influences. We need to look at how these conditions have shaped a regional architecture over time.

Building and architecture have an interactive relationship with nature. More than many regions, however, the Pacific Northwest has always had a close association with the natural world. This ecoregion-based design, in which architects exploit the great power of the landscape, has been a constant, with an ongoing search for expression through a free and open relationship to nature and place.

THE PACIFIC NORTHWEST REGION

The Pacific Northwest is a relatively isolated bioregion in North America. Referred to by ecologists as Cascadia, and by biologists as the Coastal Temperate Rain Forest Zone, it stretches from southeastern Alaska to northern California, from the Pacific Ocean to the crest line of the Cascade Range. Rain forests are distinguished by high precipitation, an equable year-round climate, proximity to oceans, presence of coastal mountains, and infrequent fires. They are among the most biologically productive places on earth. Although Cascadia represents less than 10 percent of the North American continent, it contributes 20–25 percent of the total surface runoff from rain.

Mountains, lowland terrain, and water are the ingredients that create spectacular landscapes. The mountains border the great saltwater sounds, inlets of the Pacific Ocean, with towering summits, steep slopes, and valleys. The mountainous terrain has created drainages of all sizes, from cascading creeks to mighty rivers. Where the rivers arrive at the tidal waters, other landforms emerge: rocky headlands, steep bluffs, tall dunes, and wooded slopes.

Until recent times, there was nearly uninterrupted forest composed of towering firs, hemlock, and cedar as well as bright green alder, maple, and an undergrowth of dense shrubs and herbs. Significant valleys with their associated rivers are carved out of these mountains and hills. British Columbia has the Fraser River Valley, with Vancouver at its mouth. In Washington, the fertile Skagit River Valley lies to the north, the central Green and Duwamish river valleys stretch to Elliott Bay near Seattle, and the mighty Columbia River Valley is located at the border with Oregon. Portland, Oregon's largest city, sits at the intersection of the Columbia and Willamette rivers. The

(Opposite) Mt. Baker. Photo: Alvin Waite

The Pacific Northwest region. Map provided by Ecotrust

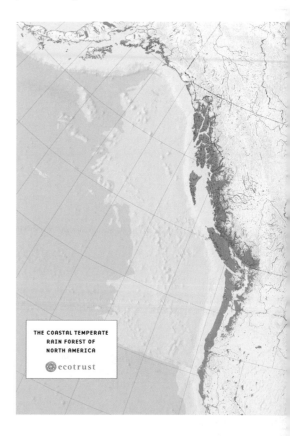

THE COASTAL TEMPERATE
RAIN FOREST OF
NORTH AMERICA

ecotrust

(Above, left) Loggers pose while felling a fir tree, Washington, 1906. Photo: Darius Kinsey (University of Washington Libraries, Special Collections, D. Kinsey A14)

(Above, right) Men encircle cedar tree, Washington. Photo: University of Washington Libraries, Special Collections, UW 2369, photographer unknown

(Opposite, top) Guy Anderson at work in his studio, Seattle, 1965. Photo: Art Hupy (University of Washington Libraries, Special Collections, HUPY 0125-10)

(Opposite, bottom) King of the Clouds. View of Mount Rainier, Washington, 1934. Photo: Kyo Koike (University of Washington Libraries, Special Collections, UW 23838)

majority of the region's economic production has occurred in these valleys, along the rivers and in the large metropolitan areas.

The cultural and economic history of the Pacific Northwest is as much about peaks and valleys as is its natural history. In the 1800s, several events precipitated a major economic expansion in the region and fueled an emerging economy: the arrival of the transcontinental railroad, with the Northern Pacific's route terminating at Tacoma; the Klondike Gold Rush in southeastern Alaska, with Seattle as its supply base; and the ever expanding shipping of vast amounts of timber out of Pacific Northwest ports.

Even with this rapid development, the Pacific Northwest in 1900 had a population of barely three-quarters of a million people and was far removed from the rest of the world. A hundred years ago, it was an isolated region. By 1945, however, the Pacific Northwest had become an important part of the world and its unfolding history. The construction of the great Grand Coulee Dam on the Columbia River, completed in 1940, and the series of downstream dams that followed nurtured extensive agricultural development in the central desert zones of Washington and Oregon.

The development of the Boeing Airplane Company in Seattle spurred the region's World War II economy at the same time that another war industry, plutonium production, emerged at Hanford, Washington. Whatever innocence remained as to the purposes of that industry vanished over Hiroshima and Nagasaki. As David Buerge poetically states in *Washingtonians*, "Washington had joined the world with a bang and dramatically come of age."[1]

After the war, as the region's wealth and power increased, the Pacific Northwest gained appeal as a place to live. New residents seemed to identify with the region's scenic beauty. In Joel Garreau's classic text *The Nine Nations of North America*, in which he tags the Pacific Northwest "nation" with the name Ecotopia, he describes the values of the people as centered on quality of life and a willingness to explore new ideas and follow their love of nature to its political and artistic conclusions in support of the environment.[2]

Out of the ferment that grew from World War II emerged new writers, painters, naturalists, philanthropists, and reformers who contributed to the special nature of the region. Most were drawn from outside the area by the lifestyle, freedom, beauty, and opportunity that the Pacific Northwest provided. The region's color, mystery, and romantic impulses were captured by artists and architects Guy Anderson, Pietro Belluschi, Henry Gay, Jacob Lawrence, and Paul Thiry. Their state of mind in the 1940s and 1950s distinguished the region and laid the groundwork for its cultural identity.

THE MARINE COASTAL CLIMATE

The even-tempered maritime climate defines life in the Pacific Northwest. Three dominating climatic controls bring the region its particular brew of daily weather: (1) the Pacific Ocean, acting as the region's thermostat and generator of moisture-laden air, (2) the semipermanent high- and low-pressure cells that hover over the North Pacific Ocean and propel maritime air in the direction of the Sound, and (3) the mountains bordering Puget Sound and the Strait of Georgia near Vancouver, which regulate the flow of regional atmosphere. The combined effect of these controls is a predict-able general climate, described as "maritime," in other words, mild and wet. Mild ocean air brings relatively warm winters to this area. Precipitation comes mainly as rain, more than 75 percent of which falls between Octo-ber 1 and March 31. It rarely rains hard and never torrentially. Snow falls very little in the lowlands; however, at higher elevations, snow precipitation greatly increases. Annual precipitation for the Puget Sound basin averages only forty inches. Every month brings some precipitation, though minimal amounts fall in July and August.[3]

From mid-October to early spring, the prevailing winds in the Pacific Northwest blow eastward from the Pacific Ocean. This brings considerable moisture, and as this air moves over the cooler land, it condenses and initi-ates the predictable rainy season. The coastal mountains exert a profound effect on the wet air borne by the westerly winds. The coastal ranges and the windward face of the Cascades deflect the eastward-moving air upward, and precipitation results. In summer, the general flow of surface air is from the north and northwest, heading east through the Strait of Juan de Fuca and down Puget Sound. Yet, despite the consistent nature of the region's climate, extremes of heat and cold, wet and dry, can occur, as can variations caused by local differences in topography. So ecology and climate are intricately interwoven, forming the essential natural forces for a regional architecture. As the renowned Vancouver architect Arthur Erickson states in his monograph:

> The Northwest Coast of North America is a particularly difficult area with its watery lights, which are capable of somber and melancholy moods. The coast demands that buildings be transparent to light, by means of walls of glass or devices like skylights to bathe the walls, or water to reflect the sky's brightness from the earth's dark surfaces.[4]

THE NORTHWEST STYLE

Northwest Regionalism in architecture has gone through four distinct phases: (1) Northwest Coast Native American, (2) Early Regional Mod-ernism, developed just prior to and after World War II, (3) the Northwest "Contemporary" Style of the 1960s and 1970s, and (4) the recent wave of Northwest Regionalism, from the early 1990s to the present. Each was

unique and developed regional architectural responses that influenced the subsequent period.

Although little remains of the Northwest Coast Native vernacular, the forms and methods of construction used by these tribal cultures responded to conditions of climate and topography in direct and elegant ways. Generally sited along the shores of saltwater sounds just above intertidal beaches, Native structures were pure, boxlike forms of cedar timbers that functioned in the secular realm as shelter and in the spiritual realm as ceremonial centers. These powerful structures were manifestations of the cosmos, much like other corresponding structures of Native American societies, such as the tepee, the pit house, and the kiva.

The wooden plank structures were primarily of two types. One is the ridgepole building with a two-pitched gable roof that is typified more characteristically by the northern coast tribes of the Haida; the other is the single-pitched, shed-roof structure commonly known as the "longhouse" among the southern Salish tribes. Each structural type was further characterized by details of construction and joinery methods. The art associated with these structures reflected the house as an abode of the living as well as of the ancestors. One entered into the body of the ancestor through the building's mouth, the oval door, which was accentuated by housefront paintings. The northern Haida structures had a frontal pole totem with the entryway in its base, which was integrated into the facade. These painted facades and carved frontal poles represented sacred animals, natural phenomena such as clouds and rainbows, and celestial bodies like the moon and stars. The powerful architectural forms of the decorated facade and the vertical totem, as well as the strong representation of the natural world in the Native artwork, have had a profound and lasting influence on the regional architecture of the Pacific Northwest.

Haida village with frontal pole totems, 1897, Kasaan, Alaska. Photo: Frank La Roche (University of Washington Libraries, Special Collections, La Roche 181)

Native Americans built these typical structures for both permanent winter villages and temporary summer dwellings. They constructed the houses so they could dismantle the structures and reuse the plank wall cladding in the next building.

During the 1920s and 1930s, when Modernism was emerging in the United States, the architects of the Pacific Northwest were still deeply entrenched in the romantic classicism of the Beaux Arts. Pacific Northwest architecture lacked individuality, reflecting the absence of demand for a local identity. It was after World War II that a generation of architects emerged to cement what we now know as the Northwest Regional Style. From the drawing boards of Paul Thiry in Seattle, John Yeon and Pietro Belluschi in Portland, and C. E. Pratt and Fred Hollingsworth in Vancouver came a more grounded, personally reflective, and localized Modernism. Thiry describes the beginnings of Modernism in the Pacific Northwest (ironically citing Le Corbusier, the great "universalist"):

Blair Kirk House, Mercer Island, Washington, by Paul Hayden Kirk, 1960. Photo: University of Washington, College of Architecture and Urban Planning

> It was a time to listen to the voice of Corbusier from across the sea; to Eliel Saarinen and his basic philosophy; to Frank Lloyd Wright and others. Time was taken to review the wonderful things Antonin Raymond was doing in Japan. With all came a reaction against things as they were generally being done and the desire to design for the country—maybe not a "machine for living" as expressed by Corbusier but rather as a building that would better fit a way of life, that would fit the land, exploit the vast panoramas of waterways and mountains that make the Northwest, that would enliven the gray days of the winter and share the exterior country in summer: Buildings that would be flexible and adaptable to an infinite variety of situations: buildings that would shed the rain, take it away from the walls, yet permit the sun to infiltrate the interior.[5]

This influential group of early Pacific Northwest modernists was followed by the hard-core champions of the Northwest School—Paul Hayden Kirk, Wendell Lovett, Victor Steinbrueck, and Roland Terry. These architects attracted international recognition as a group of strong designers who were creating an architecture inflected by landscape, open, light filled, and above all disciplined in plan and section. This work was manifested not in large institutional and commercial buildings but in structures with small, simple programs on beautiful sites. Houses, churches, small office buildings, community libraries, and clinics were all articulated by a wood-frame post-and-beam style, in-filled with glass, and embodied a rigorous attention to detail.

This unique interpretation of international Modernism was recognized in June 1953 by the American Institute of Architects when it held its national convention in Seattle. Numerous articles followed in national and international architectural publications featuring the work of prominent Pacific Northwest architects. In 1959, Wendell Lovett was invited to the Congrès Internationaux d'Architecture Moderne (CIAM) in Europe to address the world's elite architectural practitioners and theorists.

These architects brought to their work a sense of equanimity, an economy of means and material, and a profound love of nature. The buildings of the Northwest Regional Style are unique to their place, nestled tightly into

Olsen Medical Clinic, Edmonds, Washington, by Paul Hayden Kirk, 1962. Photo: Dearborn-Masser (University of Washington Libraries, Special Collections, DM 02497)

the land and well adapted to the region's climatic conditions. The built structures did not compete with nature in terms of regional identity, and the design work of this period represents some of the finest American examples of a symbiotic relationship between architecture and its local environment.

Lovett vacation house, Crane Island, Washington, by Wendell Lovett, 1971. Photo: Christian Staub

CHAPTER 2

SUSTAINABLE DESIGN IN THE PACIFIC NORTHWEST: A BRIEF HISTORY

This chapter will address aspects of environmental design in relation to the history of architecture in the Pacific Northwest. This rich and complex architectural story begins with the earliest Pacific Coast Salish villages, includes the rapid development of the region's cities in the late 1800s, and discusses a series of early modernist periods—from the Arts and Crafts era, the International Style of the Depression and World War II, and the Northwest regional Modernism of the 1960s—through several stylistic iterations of Modernism, and into the present. Each period has made distinct contributions to the development of environmental architecture in the Pacific Northwest.

When one investigates the work of the important architects of the Pacific Northwest, it becomes clear that many qualities of the region's architecture that are appreciated by today's designers integrate a serious environmental dimension into the work. We can even trace the green architectural lineage back to the coastal indigenous structures of Native Americans. This environmental history is unique and powerful and should be recognized as a significant chapter in the development of an international sustainable-design movement.

Although the terms "sustainability" and "green" gained currency in the 1980s and 1990s, their precepts have a much longer history. To fully discuss the environmental aspects of the work of Pacific Northwest architects, it is necessary to define what is meant by "green" as applied here and also to place some limits on the range of issues to be tackled within such a definition.

The word "green" and the term "sustainable design" have enormous scope when applied to the field of architecture. At one end of the spectrum are the larger planning and policy questions as well as related concerns of social and economic sustainability. However, because this book focuses on how a designer might arrive at a position on meaningful and appropriate architectural form, these wider socioeconomic issues, which are fundamental to the future of our planet, will be set aside. At the other, purely architectural end are issues that involve a building's siting, shape, and size; materiality; embodied and recurring energy loads; longevity and maintenance; recycling or reuse; and contribution to local biodiversity and microclimate. These issues have subsets, such as the type of building program, space efficiency, sustainable properties of local materials and resources, active versus passive energy strategies, and construction systems that accommodate adaptability and site conditions, including environmental water management and control of the water cycle.

When an architect confronts these choices during the design process, various strategies begin to shape the form and conceptual approach of buildings. Today, many of these strategies are objective and quantifiable,

(Opposite) Cedar trees had many uses in Pacific Coast Salish culture. The canoes and structures shown here were made from cedar on Prince of Wales Island in southern Alaska. Photo: Underwood and Underwood (University of Washington Libraries, Special Collections, Viola Garfield Collection, NA 3601)

such as the use of daylight to reduce electric lighting loads, the design of the skin of a building relative to heat gain and loss, the use of ventilation strategies to offset the need for mechanical ventilation and reduce indoor air pollution, the employment of earth-sheltering methods or green roofs to reduce heat loss and conserve water, the utilization of low-embodied-energy materials, and the use of local resources. There are also more subjective strategies that contribute to the physical and psychological comfort of buildings. All of these issues and strategies are interwoven in a rich tapestry of opportunities and challenges for a designer. A diagram of the issues and strategies and their connections would be formidable.

The green architectural spectrum is a broad and overlapping one that tends to become more difficult as the size of the structure and the complexity of the urban context increase. Balancing energy conservation with environmental health for a building's occupants is another concern, and one of great debate. Manuscripts on sustainable design frequently emphasize the energy issue and ignore or touch only lightly on the environmental well-being of people.

Green design can address these matters in many ways. A process of design that integrates these complex strategies is at the same time scientific and intuitive—the scientific approach leans toward technological strategies and the intuitive approach toward the spiritual. Both approaches are valid and necessary when designing a truly sustainable project.

As mentioned earlier, today's designers benefit on the scientific side from a vast array of technological design tools as well as sophisticated systems and materials. Emphasis on the scientific has focused the discussion on the technical design issues of energy and building performance. In a sense, architects miss the point when they remain focused on resources-related matters when the larger criteria are tied to the health of the individual and the natural environment. Early modernist architects maximized the occupant's sense of comfort with simple and elegant architectural strategies. By increasing transparency with more glass in a building's exterior skin, compacting the footprint with the development of the open plan, and opening the building's interior to the exterior, the new architecture directly improved health. These intuitive design strategies that were so successful in making buildings full of light, space, and air remind us that there is an environmental dimension to all human activities.

"Sustainability" is often described by Douglas S. Kelbaugh, dean of the College of Architecture and Urban Planning at the University of Michigan, as having a triple bottom line—the "Three E's" of environmental, economic, and (social) equity. Although this book focuses on the environmental, especially as it relates to architectural design, there is a fourth "E," the esthetic, which is very relevant. If a building is not beautiful, it won't be loved; it won't be maintained and kept. In short, it will not be sustained.[1]

An historical perspective on the environmental architecture of the Pacific Northwest reveals an early emphasis on the intuitive, with scientific strategies coming into the picture only after 1970. The intuitive design solutions that have a strong environmental emphasis were not entirely unconscious, however. A real consciousness of designing for the environment has long been an integral aspect of Pacific Northwest architecture. It can be seen in the Arts and Crafts–influenced houses of Washington architects Kirtland Cutter and Elsworth Storey, designed at the beginning of the twentieth

The Buckley Residence, Seattle, by Paul Hayden Kirk, expresses the qualities of early Northwest Modernism. Photo: Dearborn-Masser (University of Washington Libraries, Special Collections, DM02095)

century. It can then be traced through a series of distinct design periods in the Pacific Northwest, when each new era was influenced by and built on the architectural philosophy of the previous generation. Design that is explicitly green tends to be expressed in episodic peaks of activity that relate to the principal periods of architectural history. The depth of environmental thinking has varied during these periods. The green "trail" will be presented mainly through the work of individual architects who have explicitly engaged with the ecological and environmental issues of their time. Within all of the periods, however, there is an overarching respect for the landscape of the region. The Pacific Northwest landscape is so pristine and beautiful that it beckons the designer to be respectful and to work with it.

NORTHWEST COAST NATIVE STRUCTURES

The history of environmental architecture in the Pacific Northwest begins several thousand years ago with the indigenous structures of the Pacific Coast Salish tribes. The simple structures of cedar planks were profoundly integrated into the physical environment and spiritual world of the Native peoples. This single material, cedar, provided generously for the needs of the culture—materially, ceremonially, and medicinally. As Hilary Stewart states in her book on cedar and its impact on the art and culture of Pacific Northwest natives:

> The marine-oriented peoples of the Northwest Coast dwelt on the fringes of the great evergreen forests and were encompassed by a mystic world of spirit beings. They held the supernatural cedar in high esteem, for, like the bountiful salmon of the sea, the ubiquitous tree of the forest gave of itself to sustain and enrich their lives.[2]

Haida villages were built to face the water. Photo: Webster & Stevens (University of Washington Libraries, Special Collections, General Indian Collection, Db 12)

Wakasham with gable roof, Kasaan, Alaska, 1915. Photo: John Thwaites (University of Washington Libraries, Special Collections, NA 3557)

Understanding the integral relationship between a single material and the culture of a community provides an important lesson in the use and conservation of local natural resources. All parts of the cedar tree were used. From the straight-grained, rot-resistant wood, men made canoes, post-and-beam houses, storage boxes, totemic memorial poles, and ceremonial masks. The smaller trunk sections and branches yielded bowls and dishes, and from the bark came baskets, clothing, bedding, and even diapers. Although the cedar tree is slow growing and not easily renewed in today's culture of consumption, the total life-sustaining, reciprocal relationship between a material and human needs inspires holistic design thinking today.

The structures of these marine-oriented peoples faced the water. They generally were lined up in a single row set slightly uphill from the water's edge. Large extended families lived together under the same roof. In this culture, the house was a home and a symbol. Inside and outside, the structures bore crest figures expressing the history and unique character of the lives of the occupants. In a sense, each house was like a base camp for a group of families who moved seasonally to alternate sites for hunting, fishing, and gathering. In winter, they returned to the base village to live out the colder months together.

The structures, all post and beam, were of two types: the shed-roof house and the gable-roof *wakasham*. In the southern region around Puget Sound, the shed-roof structures were more common. In the northern region along the British Columbia shores, the *wakasham* was the dominant type.

The two Coastal Native house types: the gable-roof four-beam *wakasham* (top) and the shed-roof house (bottom). Drawings from Native American Architecture *by Peter Nabokov and Robert Easton*

(Bottom) Detail of wall with lapped cedar planks. Photo: University of Washington Libraries, Special Collections, NA 1818, photographer unknown

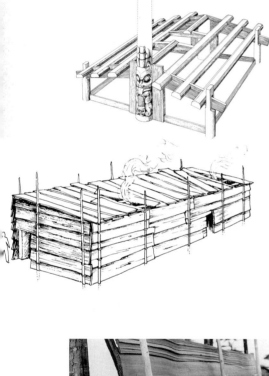

The shed-roof houses provide us with many interesting lessons in designing for the Pacific Northwest environment. These structures had two rows of posts, with the seaward side set slightly higher than the forest side. Made completely of western red cedar, they had removable roofs and walls made of large planks. The pairs of posts were arranged in regular bays, with the number variable to determine the size of the structure. The depth was fairly constant, set by the span of the crossbeams. The crossbeams supported purlins, which then supported the wide roof planks. The planks had lipped edges and were interlocked like tiles. They allowed both expansion, to accommodate larger or additional families, and dismantling, so that the walls and roof could be transported to other sites. The posts remained in place for the return and reinstallation of the cladding components. These plain forms with their highly adaptable structural systems and beautifully crafted timber-plank skins, often regarded as some of the most elegant indigenous structures in North America, serve as excellent examples of sustainable design.

The regular, modular forms of the indigenous peoples of the Pacific Northwest blurred the differences between the dwellings of the chiefs or aristocracy and the common tribal members. The structures were regular, repetitive, and unself-conscious. They were integrated with the environment through their appropriateness to human scale, use of local materials, and craftsmanship, not necessarily by blending into nature. In fact, these structures stood proudly on the shoreline, their artfully painted facades expressing the history and spirit of each village. This combination of good ecological fit, construction craft, and goal of material economy, together with a strong concern for embellishment of the tribe's cosmology, created a sensuous frugality that resulted in elegance.

We may also learn lessons in climate-responsive design from Northwest Coast Native peoples. Given the relatively temperate climate, with mild winters and cool summers, achieving comfort required a modest amount of heat in both seasons. As wood was the primary heating source in these structures, the full potential of the biomass was exploited. Timber has a high resistance to the flow of heat and a low thermal capacity. The latter means that a timber building will warm up quickly when heated.

Ventilation techniques were quite sophisticated in these structures as well. The narrow footprint with minimum partitions that typically did not extend to the roof facilitated cross ventilation from breezes coming off the water. The walls generally were constructed of lapped flat planks slung horizontally between vertical posts. These were tied with cedar bark twine, thus creating natural air gaps. A narrow slot at the base of the wall offered additional ventilation. Openings in the walls that might have allowed for light and views were kept at a minimum in order to decrease heat loss in the winter months. A single hole in the center of the roof allowed smoke from the interior fire pits to exit and also served as another ventilation outlet. These houses had bare soil floors and often an excavated center area that could be used as a social gathering zone around the fire. Many of the larger Haida dwellings had deeply excavated house pits, which descended in stages and took advantage of the heat captured from the earth's median temperature.

These remarkable structures, which were highly adaptable, naturally heated, and ventilated and made use of every part of the sacred cedar trees, present us with superior environmental design lessons. The simple, graceful forms, completely responsive to conditions of place and culture, have also inspired Pacific Northwest architects for many generations.

THE ARTS AND CRAFTS PERIOD

Although the Arts and Crafts period in the Pacific Northwest was not nearly as notable as it was in California or as expressed in the New England Shingle Style, it produced some significant if modest structures with interesting environmental aspects. Elsworth Storey, who practiced in Seattle from 1905 until 1945, and Carl Gould, whose Seattle practice spanned the years from 1909 until his death in 1934, created some extremely innovative houses. Kirtland Kelsey Cutter, from Spokane, who produced several noteworthy projects in Seattle and was for a time Washington State's leading architect, also made a significant contribution to early Northwest regional architecture. The work of these early regionalists made straightforward use of modest materials and standard sawmill-run timber. The residential projects of Elsworth Storey were some of the first in the country to explore ideas of building very lightly on the land with post-and-beam structural frames.

Although styles were for the most part imported during this period, the best work of the era showed adaptations to the Pacific Northwest environment that began to develop a localized architectural response. In 1933, A. H. Albertson stated in an article published in the *Town Crier*, which contained a collection of essays by a number of Seattle architects:

Tlingit interior fire pit. Photo: W. H. Partridge (University of Washington Libraries, Special Collections, NA 2547)

(Bottom) Seattle Golf and Country Club, by Kirtland Cutter. Photo: University of Washington Libraries, Special Collections, UW 14763

(Above) Bainbridge Island residence by Carl Gould. Photo: William Booth

(Right) Colman Park cottages by Elsworth Storey. Photo: Art Hupy

We still may express distinctive local culture in our architectural forms. In fact, I believe a sensitive interpretation of our environment will impel us to do so . . . irrespective of outside influences and traditions. We have the mountains . . . we have the change in color and shades of the waters [and we have] the colonnades and cathedrals of the forest.[3]

Some of the earliest Arts and Crafts buildings to display qualities of a distinctly Pacific Northwest architecture were designed by Kirtland Cutter. Although possibly influenced by the Bay Area School, which included Bernard Maybeck, Cutter's half-timbered houses in the North Seattle Highlands and his Seattle Golf and Country Club building emphasize broad eaves, fine craftsmanship, and simple details. Many of Cutter's houses, although fairly eclectic in style, had finely integrated gardens and fully glazed sunrooms and inglenooks. These architectural appendages were an early attempt to draw the region's natural landscape into the interior space.

Storey's rental cottages, built as a speculative development at Colman Park in Seattle, are fine examples of modest structures that fit into a natural landscape. These six small houses, sited in a loosely aligned row, terrace down the hillside in a large park designed by the Olmsted Brothers. The footprints are small, and each structure has a porch under the extended gable roof. Parking is in a remote parking area along Lake Washington Boulevard South, with footpaths to the individual houses—much like the current cohousing projects that have become popular in the Pacific Northwest. University of Washington professor Grant Hildebrand states in his essay in *Shaping Seattle Architecture:*

These are textbook examples of the elegant coordination of modest materials. These cottages, together with the Evans house and the two Storey houses, have been most influential for later designers, perhaps because, in their fresh underivative forms and their thoughtfully imaginative use of simple local materials, they have been seen as his most original interpretations of building in the Puget Sound region.[4]

The Bainbridge Island, Washington, residence by Carl Gould, built in 1914–15 for his family, employed a light post-and-beam structure similar to that of the Storey cottages. However, rather than in-filling the frame with vertical cedar siding as Storey had, Gould fully glazed the frames with multiple windows. The entire structure was effectively turned into a giant sunroom. Even more innovative was the modular construction, which utilized a wall panel system prefabricated off-site and barged to the island (Gould used the same system in the marine laboratory building on San Juan Island, Washington). These two residential projects predated the use of architecture of the systems-pavilion type used in the West Coast Case Study houses. In the Pacific Northwest, however, the Arts and Crafts work that explored the use of systems and standardized construction never allowed the architectural tectonics to dominate the natural qualities of a site.

Lovell Residence, Los Angeles, by Richard Neutra. Photo: University of Washington College of Architecture and Urban Planning

EARLY NORTHWEST MODERNISTS

What the Arts and Crafts period started, with the integration of a romantic architecture of place with fine timber craftsmanship, the early Northwest modernists expanded, with their articulated post-and-beam designs.

In the late 1920s, several important events occurred that pushed the Modern Movement toward a series of theoretical and environmental positions. In 1927, Le Corbusier published his *Towards a New Architecture* in English, and the Weissenhofsiedlung was built in Stuttgart, Germany, with notable buildings by Le Corbusier, Walter Gropius, Mies van der Rohe, and other leading figures. Also that year, Richard Neutra broke ground in Los Angeles on the Health House, for Dr. P. M. Lovell, and Buckminster Fuller published his initial sketches for the Dymaxion House. These leading protagonists had embarked on bold constructional experiments, and the work had a profound effect on a generation of architects.

When the Modern Movement reached the Pacific Northwest in the late 1920s and 1930s, the region's architects were extremely influenced by the radical new ideas. The new modern architecture was considered the most effective instrument of the "good society" and found receptive eyes and ears in the cultural environment of idealism in the undeveloped West. The rapidly expanding population and the associated building boom combined to meet at exactly the right moment with a fertile cadre of architectural practitioners, the intriguing concepts of Modernism, and the search for a new style to fit a new land, and a truly regional expression began to develop. The Pacific Northwest architects who gained renown at this time were Pietro Belluschi and John Yeon, in Portland; Lister Holmes, Lionel Pries, and Paul Thiry, in Seattle; and Robert A. D. Berwick, C. E. Pratt, and Peter Thornton, in Vancouver. These eager, young designers had been trained in the Beaux-Arts tradition but were ready and willing to cross over to the International Style.

The radical ideals of the movement's leading figures, broadcast to an international audience of architects and students of architecture via their writings, pushed these newly indoctrinated Northwest modernists toward inventive forms and solutions. These solutions had a strong environmental bent brought about by a respect for the natural landscape but also by the tectonic language of the International Style buildings, which were receiving worldwide press.

The environmental bent of these seminal figures is examined in Colin Porteous's recent publication *The New Eco-Architecture: Alternatives from the Modern Movement.* Porteous's position is that there is a green past in the heroic period of early Modernism that is relevant to the present. His wide range of examples, delineating radical experimentation with environmental solutions by many early modernists, illustrates the profound influence these designers had with respect to these issues. In discussing Le Corbusier's architectural control over microclimate, Porteous quotes his explanation of the verdant patios at Maison Curutchet:

> I insist: the hanging garden seems to me the modern formula for a practical intake of fresh air, close to the centre of family life; one walks on it with dry feet, avoiding rheumatism, sheltered from the vertical sun and from rain. . . . This garden for taking in air, multiplied along vast blocks of buildings, is in fact a real sponge for air.[5]

Following the lead of the key figures of the International Style, the Northwest modernist architects of this early period adopted their own regional environmental strategies. A regional variation on these principles was to be expected; however, the localized environmental approaches were pervasive and were tied so directly to the formal expression of the regional architecture that they are unique models and worthy of close examination.

Modernist principles did not appear to any extent in the Pacific Northwest until the 1930s work of Paul Thiry. Thiry, who practiced in Seattle from

Kerry House, 1938, Seattle, by Paul Thiry. Photo: Richard Garrison

1929 to 1977, studied at the University of Washington in the late 1920s and at the American School of Paris in Fontainebleau. In 1934, he traveled around the world, meeting Antonin Raymond in Japan and visiting Europe a second time, where he met Le Corbusier. He was deeply influenced by the ideas of these two men and returned to Seattle with a totally new philosophy of design. At that time, he talked about an architecture that was not exactly Le Corbusier's "machine for living" but rather one that would fit the land, exploit the vast panoramas of waterways and mountains, enliven the gray days of winter, and share the outdoors in summer. He spoke of an architecture that would be flexible and adapt to an infinite variety of situations: buildings that would shed rain and take it away from the walls yet permit the sun to infiltrate the interior.

Thiry's early residential designs were greatly influenced by the International Style, utilizing flat roofs and cubic stucco forms with minimum detail. These rigorous forms were marked by large expanses of glass for bringing in abundant light and always had a close relation to a garden. His Kerry House in Seattle, built in 1938, shows a more sympathetic relationship to its site than does the early cubist work.

In Portland, a parallel but somewhat more unique regional style was developing. This eclectic style drew from many sources—Modernism, obviously, but also the California Stick Style and rural vernacular barns and utilitarian farm structures. The two leading figures were Pietro Belluschi and John Yeon.

Belluschi's architecture was a more personal approach to architectural form compared to those of other Pacific Northwest architects practicing in the modernist style. Belluschi immigrated to the United States from Italy and studied at Cornell University. Following his architectural education, he settled in Portland in the 1920s. Largely undeveloped at the time, Oregon's landscape was vastly different from that of Italy and made a strong impression on Belluschi. His architecture was distinguished by its strong partnership with the landscape and his attention to the qualities of the region's

(Top) Kerr House, Gearhart, Oregon, by Pietro Belluschi. Photo: Meredith Clausen

Kerr House. Photo: Meredith Clausen

Plan of Watzek House, Portland, by John Yeon. Drawing courtesy of Oregon Historical Society

(Bottom) Watzek House courtyard. Photo: Meredith Clausen

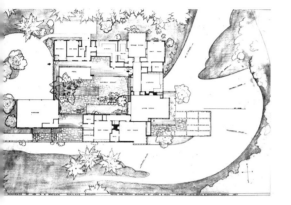

light. His houses in particular took a backseat to the drama of the site. A bench in Portland's Forest Park bears a plaque with a quote from Belluschi: "A house can never be as beautiful as a tree."

Two of the most representative houses of Belluschi's site-sensitive architecture built during the early modernist period are the Sutor House (1937–38), in Portland, and the Kerr House (1941), in Gearhart, Oregon. These two houses are both organic and ordered, elegant yet raw, deferring to the grace and beauty of the landscape. They are uncomplicated rectangular forms with pure gable roofs and monochromatic wood exteriors. The entrance vestibule of the Sutor House is like a Japanese pavilion, with full-length plate glass windows, mat floors, and a fir-wood ceiling.

The Kerr House, a vacation home on the Oregon dunes, is an important work of Pacific Northwest residential architecture that has had a lasting influence on generations of architects. At the time it was designed, modern architecture was in its infancy and was not attentive to regional character. Built on an expanse of wild exposed coast, the low-lying linear form nestles into its site in a quiet yet tough stance. The house contains qualities of "rooted" architecture espoused by Christian Norberg-Schultz and, together with the Watzek House by John Yeon, made a significant contribution to an emerging regional style.

The Watzek House in Portland, designed by John Yeon while he was working in the office of another important Portland architect, Albert E. Doyle, is a beautiful piece of early modernist work. Designed for a prominent

businessman and civic leader, Aubrey Watzek, and his mother, the house
is sited in a roughly U-shape configuration around a central courtyard. This
site approach facilitates a natural ventilation scheme with all the major
public spaces opening onto the garden court. Meredith Clausen describes
the house in her book *Pietro Belluschi: Modern American Architect*:

> Starkly modern, elegant yet frankly of wood, formal yet one with the
> natural terrain, it sat low on the horizon, a single-story structure of
> conventional wood frame construction with flush siding. . . . a meticu-
> lously controlled formal order of clearly articulated triangulated forms
> and staggered roof lines balanced by slim columns and chimneys.
> Conceived less as a functional building than a perfect work of art, it
> revealed a painter's eye at work, now in three dimensions and on an
> architectural scale.[6]

Yeon had an intense interest in order and formal rigor. The Watzek
House features very distinct spaces in a formal hierarchy that links axially
and gathers natural light into the interior.

This concern for precision in composition carried over into an interest in economy and engineering. Yeon was a proponent of the systems
approach to design and created a group of modular plywood houses. In
these innovative structures, windows were set between the studs, with no
operable panes. Ventilation was provided by a series of louvers beneath
the windows. Yeon admired Frank Lloyd Wright but strove to make his work
calmer, serene, and, as he described it, "not scratchy."

In Vancouver, a group of architects closely associated with artist B. C.
Binning were designing houses using elements of contemporary European
Modernism. Architects Robert A. D. Berwick and C. E. Pratt collaborated
with Binning on his own house in West Vancouver. Developed as a model
for the ordinary market, the house was an inexpensive structure with an

Wallace Lovett Residence, Bellevue, Washington, by Wendell Lovett. Photo: Dearborn-Masser (University of Washington Libraries, Special Collections, DM 02877)

open plan and a strong relationship between internal and external space.

Although the influence was great, distance and the unique landscape of the Pacific Northwest tempered the European Modernism that prevailed internationally. The legendary power of the landscape as well as the lack of historical layering that Europe was forcefully rejecting aided the development of a more regional version of the new International Style. It is important to note, however, that despite the respect for the landscape that permeated the work of these new modernists, the larger projects, such as Belluschi's superb Equitable Building in downtown Portland (1932), showed little regional influence. Instead, the emerging Northwest style was manifested in the everyday world of housing, schools, churches, and small office and commercial projects. This can be seen especially in the next wave of modernist architects in the Pacific Northwest.

THE NORTHWEST SCHOOL

The second generation of Northwest modernists is represented by a collection of relatively small offices working in a remarkably similar style. By 1945, many of the key architects practicing in the Puget Sound region, the Portland metropolitan area, and Vancouver had been born and reared in the region and understood its climate and history. Fueled by a prolific postwar building boom, the old ideas of past forms had been rejected and replaced with a strikingly consistent brand of regionalism. A few of the architects of the early modernist period, chiefly Pietro Belluschi and Paul Thiry,

bridged the war times and continued to make significant contributions to the work of the emerging Northwest School. Practitioners and students alike were enthusiastic about the new style of architectural work being created in the Pacific Northwest. This overall enthusiasm generated a strong bond within the design community that spread beyond the field of architecture. The art community as well as important writers and politicians were caught up in the energy of the new regional identity.

Two institutions, one academic and one professional, became active forums for this architecture and promoted its ideas. From the 1930s and through the 1960s, the academic environment at the University of Washington's Department of Architecture provided a catalyst for the theories of the Northwest School. Central to these theories was Professor Lionel Pries, whose teachings influenced many of the best architects of this period, including Fred Bassetti, Paul Kirk, Victor Steinbrueck, Roland Terry, and Gene Zema.

The other institution that played a major role in promoting this Northwest regional architecture was the Seattle chapter of the American Institute of Architects (A.I.A.). While the rest of the country was beginning to recognize the Northwest Regional Style as unique, the institute decided to hold its national convention in Seattle in June 1953. Many important Pacific Northwest buildings were subsequently published in major architectural journals. The A.I.A. and the region's architecture schools fostered an almost moralistic stance on the simplicity and honesty of these new structures. Wendell Lovett, a professor of architecture at the University of Washington, even carried the "gospel" to Europe, speaking at the ninth meeting of the Congrès Internationaux d'Architecture Moderne in July 1959.

What were the elements and character of this new work? While the early modernists established a regionally based version of the International Style, the Northwest School articulated a wood-frame, post-and-beam style that treated the indigenous material as the only logical construction unit. Although these architects employed the glass expanses characteristic of modern architecture, such use made sense in relation to the mild climate and extraordinary natural sites.

(Above, left) Kirk residence, Seattle, by Paul Hayden Kirk. Photo: College of Architecture and Urban Planning

(Above, right) Florence Terry Residence, Seattle, by Roland Terry. Photo: Dearborn-Masser (University of Washington Libraries, Special Collections, DM 14)

(Opposite, bottom) Wallace Lovett Residence. Photo: Dearborn-Masser (University of Washington Libraries, Special Collections, DM 02885)

Buckley Residence, Seattle, by Paul Hayden Kirk. Photo: Dearborn-Masser (University of Washington Libraries, Special Collections, DM 02099)

(Bottom) Group Health Cooperative Clinic, Seattle, by Paul Hayden Kirk. Photo: Dearborn-Masser (University of Washington Libraries, Special Collections, DM 02300)

(Opposite, top) Courtyard of Putnam Residence, Seattle, by Paul Hayden Kirk. Photo: Dearborn-Masser (University of Washington Libraries, Special Collections, DM 02533)

This era of architectural design, from around 1945 until the late 1960s, had more than just a strong sense of site design. The work took a real environmental and social position that provides us with important lessons today. The elements that we see as relevant to environmental design can be described through the physical or phenomenological qualities of the Pacific Northwest landscape: earth, sky, water, and air.

There are almost always hills or mountains in the Pacific Northwest. The region's topography is both a challenge and an opportunity, and post-and-beam construction accommodates this variation. The sloped surface is the given; the flat site is the exception.

The sky is mostly gray. From October until June, the Pacific Northwest is cast in an even, milky, consistent light, sometimes called "oyster light," which magnifies the deep green of the natural landscape. It is not a transient condition; it is the dominant one. At the same time, the region's overcast sky can be bright and must be modulated by the architecture. Complementing this condition, the architecture is a subdued form with muted colors, attached to the site and subservient.

The sky of the Pacific Northwest would be oppressive without the beauty of the water as counterbalance. Water, pervasive throughout the landscape, is the region's most vital resource. It provides recreation, electrical power, and spiritual sustenance. It encompasses not only the standing water of lakes, rivers, streams, and sound but the glitter and sparkle of rain-washed surfaces in the built and natural worlds.

The region's air, like its light, is soft. Winds rarely blow with force, whereas gentle breezes are fairly constant. Given the temperate climate, the correct orientation can provide a structure with the necessary air changes naturally, thereby saving energy.

The unique conditions of these natural elements make the Pacific Northwest an excellent place for experimenting with architectural forms. The principal protagonists of the Northwest School understood these key physical factors of the landscape and climate and used them to advantage. They did not try to outmuscle the natural systems but instead adopted an architecture that shelters people in a sustainable way. The houses, schools, small

office buildings, and community structures were some of the best regional architecture in America. The forms were kept simple and refined, designed without stylistic formula, and determined by local environmental conditions and the use of native materials.

Most architectural historians associate Paul Hayden Kirk with the Northwest School. Kirk's design work—mainly homes, medical clinics, libraries, and churches of residential scale—was of wood. He studied Japanese architecture extensively and was attracted by the small, intimate gardens as well as the use of modular construction systems with expressed structure. One cannot look at the work of the Northwest School and not see the Japanese connection. Its post-and-beam architecture sits above the ground rather than digging itself into the earth. Typically, the wood is unpainted, and structural members are revealed both on the interior and the exterior. Nature is invited in. As Teiji Itoh states in *The Elegant Japanese House: Traditional Sukiya Architecture:*

Detail of Putnam Residence. Photo: Dearborn-Masser (University of Washington Libraries, Special Collections, DM 02531

> A notable characteristic of the Japanese building is in the unusual breadth of its eaves. Functionally, these broad eaves serve the purpose of protecting the building from destructive weathering and of helping to adjust the atmospheric conditions inside—for instance by providing shade in summer. At the same time, in a perhaps more psychological

Wood Research House, by Paul Hayden Kirk, Bellevue, Washington. Photo: College of Architecture and Urban Planning

(Bottom, left) The Faculty Club, University of Washington, Seattle, by Paul Hayden Kirk and Victor Steinbrueck. The building is set on a steep slope. Photo: Dearborn-Masser (University of Washington Libraries, Special Collections, DM 02664)

(Bottom, right) Faculty Club courtyard. Photo: Dearborn-Masser (University of Washington Libraries, Special Collections, DM 02672)

than physical sense, the broad eaves and the area under them serve to unite architecture with nature.[7]

From 1943 until the mid-1970s, Kirk's architecture received a great amount of national press in professional journals. During the war, he practiced with the firm Stuart, Kirk and Durham, where he designed the High Point School, in Seattle. This elegantly simple one-story structure was the first of many light-frame institutional projects. His Group Health Cooperative Clinic in the Northgate area of Seattle, completed in 1957, was an exceptional structure of repetitive post-and-beam bays with an interior garden courtyard.

Kirk's residential architecture had a strong sense of the International Style, with large glass planes from floor to ceiling that act as walls, windows, and often doors. Like the Northgate clinic, these houses were typically of post-and-beam construction and often incorporated a courtyard. They floated above the site, allowing the topography and vegetation to flow under the structure, merging it with the land. Kirk's earliest house of

note was the Blair Kirk House, completed in 1951. "This precisely detailed house translates the International Style into a Pacific Northwest wood idiom," as David Rash states in *Shaping Seattle Architecture*.[8]

Kirk's Putnam Residence, designed in the early 1950s, was unabashedly modern yet took a quiet and deferential position toward its site. It shows an amazing transparency that brings in natural light and maximizes cross ventilation. The public spaces face the garden in a straightforward L-shaped plan, maximizing privacy. The project displays Kirk's strong sense of proportion and composition that beautifully complements the Pacific Northwest landscape.

In the late 1950s and early 1960s, Kirk experimented with modular, prefabricated construction. This work was very innovative and demonstrated his keen interest in the economies of systems architecture. Kirk saw prefab technology as a means to making quality design a part of the everyday housing market. His Wood Research House, sponsored by the Weyerhaeuser Company and the Andersen Corporation, was the most inventive of these buildings. This structure took full advantage of the developing laminate-wood technology. The roof and floor were supported off four X-shape columns of laminated wood. Needing only four footings for the foundation, the system could accommodate the most uneven sites without grading. The four quadrants of the roof were hyperbolic paraboloid "trees" made of curved sections of plywood stretched over wood framing. Floors were plywood-sheathed panels, and the walls were made of precut wood siding and used stock windows. The 1,600-square-foot house designed for a family of four was built for $20,000 in 1960. By utilizing technology, this project took on many elements of residential architecture—the space plan, section, and details of construction. As an attempt to conserve the environment, it addressed a changing society's perception of the ideal house, thereby promoting a new model of living.

In the same year, 1960, the Faculty Club was completed on the University of Washington campus. Designed collaboratively by Seattle architects Paul Kirk and Victor Steinbrueck, it is considered by many to be the best example of institutional construction by architects of the Northwest School. Set on a sloping, forested site and somewhat isolated from other campus buildings, the Faculty Club was not designed in the collegiate gothic style of the central campus. Instead, the architects sought to create a residential-scale building that was open to the landscape and filled with natural light, a more intimate structure that would bring the faculty together. The building, with its simple open plan set around a courtyard that surprisingly opens to a lower level, is a polyvalent structure that accommodates small, intimate gatherings and large campus functions at the same time. This building not only is a fine example of the post-and-beam style of its time but is also an excellent model for sustainable design by today's standards.

Economy was a basic consideration for the building, as the faculty paid two-thirds of the construction cost. The post-and-beam structural system allowed the program to be laid out on the site with minimum foundations while preserving almost all the mature evergreen trees. In placing the building on the steep site in a two-story terrace, the architects took full advantage of the view and at the same time tucked the parking under the dining room. The project utilized a minimal amount of material and has the feel of a California Case Study House, with its unprotected steel structure of wide-

(Top) Richard Lea House, Lopez Island, Washington, by Lionel Pries. Photo: Victor Steinbrueck

Florence Terry Residence, Seattle, by Roland Terry. Photo: Photo: Dearborn-Masser (University of Washington Libraries, Special Collections, DM 20)

flange columns and beams. Many of the windows are designed with operable sashes, while broad overhangs and steel trellis elements shade the glazing, thus making air conditioning unnecessary. The courtyard carved into the center of the mass assists with natural airflow to most of the building's public space.

Kirk's mentor was Lionel Pries. In the late 1940s and 1950s, Pries spent most of his time teaching in the Department of Architecture at the University of Washington; he built only a few commissions during this time. These buildings displayed remarkable artistic creativity and inspired his best students, who went on to become the masters of this distinctive regional style. His Richard Lea House, built in 1947 on Lopez Island, Washington, is a remarkable design. It was one of the first contemporary buildings in the West to incorporate a sod roof.

With its low-lying mass sited parallel to the beach, this home is a truly sustainable building because it starts with nature. It merges with the rock and flora of the island's landscape as if it had grown there. The south facade is almost fully glazed so as to capture valuable natural light, maximize views, and warm the interior space. The north facade contains limited glazing, minimizing heat loss and protecting the structure from harsh northern winds. Designed just after World War II, this project, with its immediacy of craft and romantic natural beauty, was remarkably ahead of its time.

Roland Terry, another innovative designer of the Northwest School, not only designed a series of remarkable residential projects but was comfortable with bringing this sensibility to commercial projects.

Also greatly influenced by Pries, Terry designed a beautiful house for his mother in 1937 with considerable advice from his teacher. His residential designs of later years often included beach logs for columns and rustic beams of heavy timber. He was fond of glazing window systems directly into the heavy post-and-beam log structure, playing the different construction scales against one another. His own summer house on Lopez Island (see chapter 3, Earth section) and the Lawrence B. Culter Residence in Vancouver (1957–58) utilize the unique palette of peeled logs, built-in furniture, and sliding window systems. Terry's eclectic style bridged the Northwest School with Asian residential interiors and British Columbian architects' use of rustic wood construction.

In the late 1950s and 1960s, the modernist Vancouver School of British Columbia was designing equally innovative regional architecture. Key figures in this group are Arthur Erickson, Fred Hollingsworth, and Ron Thom. Once again, it is residential architecture that displays the strongest sense of a regional style. Building in the muscular landscape of British Columbia, with its extremely mountainous terrain, the work of these architects exemplifies an attitude of minimal site modification. There is also a very strong understanding of the potential of wood construction systems and a desire to integrate the physical making of buildings with natural elements of climate and topography.

The early work of Arthur Erickson, when he was in partnership with Geoffrey Massey, is some of the best of this regional school. Two houses for the same client, Mr. and Mrs. Gordon Smith, are powerful examples of the integration of site and architecture.

The modernist architects of the Northwest School and the Vancouver School wove together elements of conceptual clarity, simplicity, and appro-

(Opposite, top) Smith Residence, West Vancouver, British Columbia, by Arthur Erickson. Photo: Ezra Stoller

Canlis Restaurant, Seattle, by Roland Terry. Photo: Dearborn-Masser (University of Washington Libraries, Special Collections, DM 04502)

priateness of form in their work. Their architecture resonated with the landscape, often bringing the site into sharper focus through careful insertion of the structure. Their highly sustainable architecture integrated a number of architectural elements of ecological value. There is still much to be learned from the work of these remarkable Pacific Northwest architects of the 1950s and 1960s. For designers working in this region, who are constantly searching for new interpretations of the relationship between architectural form and the environment, it is important to understand the key elements of the work of this period:

- The use of local natural wood and stone as principal construction materials
- A great concern for blending the building with its site
- The integration of the outdoors with the structure, usually post and beam
- The use of skylights and clerestory windows as a dramatic way of bringing light into the interior
- The intricate use of exposed wood structure as an expressed decorative element
- The open plan as a means to maximize natural light within the interior

Eppich Residence, West Vancouver, British Columbia, by Arthur Erickson. Photo: Simon Scott

•Gardens and courtyard space as a continuation of the interior
architecture

THE NORTHWEST CONTEMPORARY PERIOD: THE 1970S

The 1970s saw a critical shift away from the strongly horizontal, modular
post-and-beam architecture of the 1950s and 1960s toward a much more
vertically proportioned volumetric composition that borrowed from many
sources. The architectural influences were less related to Modernism and
had more to do with the vernacular structures of the region.

At this time, architects thought of themselves as part of a larger world,
and "regionalism" was mostly a West Coast phenomenon. As in the
San Francisco Bay area, modern architecture reflected an awareness of
anonymous structures—barns, lumber mills, fish canneries, and mining
structures—long before the value of preserving these buildings was part of
public consciousness.

In the Pacific Northwest, a new generation of architects was extremely
influenced by Sea Ranch, on the coast of northern California. These architects approached their discipline as a more eclectic composition of forms,
mixing single-slope and gable-roof boxes with barnlike shed attachments for
bay windows and porches. The Tulalip Bay Community Center (1974), by
the Bumgardner Partnership, Seattle, was a large shed-roof wooden building with heavy timber structural framing. Architect Thomas Bosworth also
employed nineteenth-century techniques of barn construction for the Pilchuck
Glass School in the Cascade foothills near Stanwood, Washington. As Sally
Woodbridge states in her 1974 article for *Progressive Architecture*:

*Pilchuck Glass School, Cascade
foothills, Washington, by Thomas
Bosworth. Photo: Tom Bosworth*

*(Bottom) Pilchuck studio. Photo: Dick
Busher*

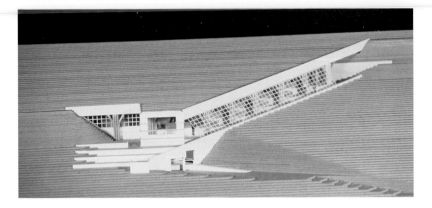

While resembling the rustic pole and shake barns built by Northwest settlers, the open-walled structure nevertheless capably accommodates glassblowers; it shelters them from rain and sun while allowing hot air from furnaces to be circulated laterally out or up through the overlap in the tiered pitches of the roof.[9]

This rustic school also incorporated small houses, built by the glassblowing instructors, as well as communal toilets and bathhouses set neatly in the woods. This highly collective living and creating environment for artists was an early model of cohousing.

Urban preservation in the 1970s was another parallel movement in Pacific Northwest architecture and involved environmental stewardship. In Seattle, a fifteen-year battle with the City of Seattle saved the historic Pike Place Market. Pioneer Square, Seattle's nineteenth-century commercial district, was also preserved at this time. Preservation efforts followed in Portland's historic core, and in Vancouver, the architectural community fought for and saved the Gastown district.

After the 1973 oil crisis, energy budgets suddenly became a major issue. In the United States, the energy crisis had set in motion a movement toward the use of solar heating and cooling techniques, including active and passive systems. Architects across the country were looking at alternative energy-saving systems that would relieve the pressure on our oil-dependent economy. Some of America's best young designers became interested in the design potential of solar architecture. A new architectural vocabulary emerged, which employed both the vernacular design principles of indigenous cultures and the newly developing technologies of the solar industry.

Many people in the Pacific Northwest took an interest in the new architectural forms of the solar movement. This was due largely to the region's cultural values, which embrace the sanctity of the natural environment, as well as the pioneering spirit that fosters willingness to try out new ideas. Since architectural form can greatly influence energy use, architects of the Pacific Northwest experimented as much with form as with systems. However, they quickly discovered that the active systems being designed for sunnier climates in the South and Southwest were not suitable for their region's cloudy weather. At the same time, architectural elements used for thermal mass in passive solar buildings, such as Trombe walls, rock storage

(Top, left) Model of the Kimmick Residence, an earth-sheltered structure, Cle Elum, Washington, by Miller/Hull. Photo: Miller/Hull

(Top, right) Sedgewick Library, University of British Columbia, Vancouver, by Rhone & Iredale Architects. Photo: Rhone & Iredale

Tulalip Bay Community Center, Tulalip Reservation, Washington, by the Bumgardner Partnership. Photo: John L. Brenneis

*(Left) Mount Angel Library interior.
Photo: Marietta Millet*

*(Right) Mount Angel Library, Saint
Benedict, Oregon, by Alvar Aalto.
Photo: Norman Johnston*

chambers, and water wall-heating systems, proved overly costly in terms of return on investment. Hybrid systems combining passive solar techniques with supplemental strategies, such as earth sheltering, sunspaces, direct gain, and natural daylighting, therefore made the most sense. Eventually, after much experimentation, many of the supplemental or sun-tempering strategies proved most effective in the milder Pacific Northwest climate.

The earth-sheltered approach combined with passive solar techniques worked well in the Pacific Northwest for many reasons. It was a natural evolution of the sod-roof residential architecture of key modernist pioneers such as Lionel Pries and Roland Terry. It also fit well with the sloping terrain and functioned efficiently in the regional climate by surrounding the structure with a stable temperature of 55–60 degrees. The Kimmick Residence designed by The Miller/Hull Partnership, Seattle, for the western slope of the Cascades integrated passive solar principles with an earth-sheltered structure. The project also utilized kit-of-parts technologies, with glazed garage door sections serving as the solar collector and structural precut peeled logs delivered to the site by a log home manufacturer.

Two college libraries were designed in this period with interesting energy-responsive strategies. The 40,000-square-foot Sedgewick Library at the University of British Columbia in Vancouver was built below an existing tree-lined mall in the heart of the campus. In order to preserve the mature oak trees, the architects, Rhone & Iredale, encased the roots and surrounding soil in brick-clad steel drums visible from the two courtyards within the project. The library substantially reduces energy costs with its earth cover.

The Mount Angel Library in Saint Benedict, Oregon, by Alvar Aalto, displays some of the best daylighting design in a public building. The reading areas are next to openings in the skin along the perimeter wall and under the skylight in the center, while the book storage area, which needs less light, is situated between the two reading areas, farthest from the pools of light.

The few buildings cited here are fine pieces of architecture that also happen to address energy problems. However, many of the experimental houses and commercial and institutional structures that grew out of the ferment associated with the solar scene had no architectural merit. The period produced many interesting design concepts and new energy codes and spawned many nonprofit organizations that took on the critical issues of rapid energy consumption and its associated environmental impact on our planet. It did not, however, produce much in the way of a truly handsome architecture. Hearts were in the right place, but eyes were not yet there.

THE 1980S TO THE NEW MILLENNIUM

If we lost our eyes for beauty in the 1970s, we lost our consciences in the 1980s and 1990s. More than ever, fashion dictated form, and architects blew through a series of styles, from Post-Modernism to Deconstructionism to Minimalism. A global view of the world dominated architectural style, and the regional perspective was lost. This obvious lack of locally based design thinking caused several architectural theorists to write on the merits of regionalism. Douglas Kelbaugh's book *Common Place,* particularly his chapter on Critical Regionalism, is an excellent treatise on these merits.[10] The culture of the Pacific Northwest, although always receptive to new ideas, takes a jaded view of trends. Fortunately, while certainly influenced by the dazzle of the new directions, the region's architectural community tended to water these styles down to an acceptable aesthetic level.

In the mid-1990s, a few architects and environmentalists realized that the excesses of the consumer-driven economies of the Western world were placing undue demands on the planet. An interest in new, sustainable-design principles took over where the solar architecture of the 1970s left off. The Pacific Northwest, always focused on the beauty of its natural environment, was particularly receptive to the idea of sustainable, eco-friendly architecture. The evolution of architectural design in the Pacific Northwest from the mid-1990s to the present is best summarized by the case studies in this book.

Courtyard of Maple Valley Library, Maple Valley, Washington, by Johnston Architects and Cutler Anderson Architects. Photo: Art Grice

CHAPTER 3

ENVIRONMENTAL STRATEGIES

The form of a building must first of all offer protection against the elements—wind, rain, heat, and cold—but the beauty and design of a building are as important as its usability and function. Only beautifully made buildings contribute to our built environment in a sustainable way and will be considered worthy of preservation. The challenge is to integrate function and aesthetic value into an enduring architecture that cooperates with nature and works in concert with ecological principles. The primary goal of sustainable design is to produce elegant architecture that utilizes a combination of the best ancient, proven building approaches and the best technological advances.

We should not expect to design buildings employing new sustainable-design strategies in the traditional design process. Sustainability is not a novel logic that we merely add to the design process. When we design buildings, the process must respect the underlying order of all living systems. The forms we conceive are really patterns, and patterns are the configurations of relationships between natural systems. As G. Z. Brown and Mark DeKay state in *Sun, Wind and Light,* architectural form is in part a manifestation of energy flows that are always present in a building. The architectural designer, by understanding the natural principles of heating, cooling, lighting, and envelope performance, can produce an integrated design. Integrated design leads to the discovery of design strategies that multiply benefits.[1]

When most architects attempt to integrate environmental technology, they first look at systems in isolation and then overlay these systems onto an architectural scheme. This approach is reinforced by the vast amount of literature on sustainable design that is organized on a systems basis. The most effective design strategies are those that are so carefully woven together that they appear seamless and read as one holistic strategy.

This chapter has been organized according to nature's most basic elements—earth, air, water, and fire—and their underlying principles and forces. This arrangement then provides a framework for integrated decision making. It concentrates on the elements and concepts of environmental design that contribute to architectural form and excludes issues that do not have formal consequences.

Looking at nature's elements helps architects and planners understand how buildings can function as organic systems, working in harmony with the biological cycles and processes of nature. Although discussed here in isolation, these elements are interdependent and interrelated. The parts of a building must create a whole, and this whole must be responsive to environmental conditions. A building affects the environment, just as the environment affects the building.

(Opposite) Reeve House, Lopez Island, Washington, by Cutler Anderson Architects. Photo: Art Grice

EARTH

The Pacific Northwest's privileged relationship with the natural world is deeply inscribed in the still-recent history that links the built environment, cities and buildings, with the land. The topographic cornucopia of mountains, lowland terrain, and water provides the fundamental ingredients of the architect's palette.

The earth should be considered in terms of siting concepts for buildings, structural responses to soil and subsoil conditions and the dynamics of earthquakes, heating and cooling principles, and habitat enhancement. Concepts of earth-sheltered design, green roofs, and landscape enhancement are all effective earth-related strategies for the Pacific Northwest.

How a building meets the land is critical. When a choice is given for the siting, topography must be considered carefully. Structures may float above the ground on columns, rest on the land, or be dug down into the earth. Regardless of the approach, one should conceive of a building as an interval in the landscape that respects the natural conditions of a place. Topography also has a significant impact on site microclimate, which has important repercussions for interior comfort.

In the Pacific Northwest, the bottom of a slope is often protected by vegetation but subject to cool, foggy night and morning conditions as cool air settles at the base of the slope. The top of a slope is the most exposed, both to the sun and to the weather. Side slopes are difficult but are frequently the dominant condition in the Pacific Northwest. They can be used to advantage when south facing, as they receive more than 100 times the solar radiation as north-facing slopes. The correct orientation can also reduce negative wind impact on a structure.

Earth-Sheltered Buildings

On sloped sites, one of the most effective environmental solutions can be to dig into the earth and construct an earth-sheltered structure. Earth sheltering may range from partially covered walls to totally covered walls and completely covered walls and roofs. These thermal flywheel strategies shield buildings from extremes of heat and cold by taking advantage of the relatively constant year-round temperature of the earth. In winter, the earth helps insulate the building, slowing heat loss, as the temperature of the earth is consistently warmer than the air temperature. In summer, the opposite occurs; the temperature of the earth is cooler than the temperature of the surrounding air and helps maintain cooler interior temperatures.

One major consideration in site planning for an earth-sheltered building is the specific location and orientation of the structure. Three factors come into play in the siting: sun, wind, and outside views. Proper orientation with respect to sun and wind produces significant energy savings, while exterior views are an important aesthetic and psychological determinant of orientation.

Although the climate of the Pacific Northwest is not typically regarded as one that supports solar design, the sun's radiant energy can be used effectively in combination with earth shelter. Available radiant heat has a great impact on site orientation of earth-sheltered design, as the window openings are likely to be concentrated on one side of the structure in order to maximize soil coverage. The best site orientation places all of the window openings on the south, with minimum glazing on the east, the west, and,

Sokol Blosser Winery, Tualatin, Oregon, by SERA Architects. Photo: Charlie Johnson

(Top, left) Earth shelter diagram of Hansen Residence, by Miller/Hull.

(Top, right) Mecry Residence, Carnation, Washington, by Miller/Hull. Photo: Ernest Braun

Lopez Island residence by Roland Terry. Photo: John Vaughan, Condé Nast Publications

particularly, the north. Although sunlight is desirable in the colder seasons, when heating is necessary, it is less desirable in the summer. Various techniques, such as vegetation and overhangs, reduce solar heat gain in the summer.

Buried buildings offer a unique opportunity to shield the structure from prevailing winds and use the earth to divert wind over the structure. An earth-sheltered design that includes a courtyard is additionally protected from wind. In summer, prevailing breezes could provide natural ventilation. Unfortunately, orienting an earth-sheltered structure so that all window openings are to the south will not create a well-ventilated building; however, there are many possible design variations that will result in good natural ventilation. (These concepts will be discussed later in detail in the Air section.)

The topography and soil conditions of a building site affect the design in a number of ways. A sloping site offers the opportunity to set an earth-covered building into the hillside. Given the varied topography of the Pacific Northwest, earth-sheltered design has had a long history in the

(Left) Fisher Pavilion, Seattle Center, by Miller/Hull. Photo: Stephen Keating

(Right) Olson residence, Longbranch, Washington, by Jim Olson. Photo: Dick Busher

region. Whether sited for passive solar gain or for preserving the natural features of a site, the Pacific Northwest probably has more beautiful earth-sheltered buildings than does any region in North America.

One of the earliest examples of sod-roof design, and still one of the most powerful site solutions in the region, is Roland Terry's summer residence on Lopez Island, in Washington's San Juan chain. Located on a south-facing hillside overlooking Fisherman's Cove, the program is split between two pavilions with a shared terrace. Rough logs, more than three feet in diameter, were pulled from the beach to make columns for the post-and-beam structure. This building emerges out of its site as an organic rampart onto a panorama that extends all the way to the horizon.

Other Pacific Northwest sod-roof houses that are beautifully integrated with their sites are Jim Olson's personal summer house in Longbranch, Washington, and Cutler Anderson's Reeve House on Lopez Island. Both are low-profile, one-story houses with narrow cross sections that maximize natural light penetration. With the Reeve House, the architects kept the 2,800-square-foot residence unobtrusive by sloping the grass-covered roof at an angle similar to the wind-shear angle of nearby weathered trees.

These three earth-sheltered houses are true sustainable models, merging so successfully with their sites that they have become profound and timeless lessons about relationships between the built and natural environments.

The recently completed Fisher Pavilion at Seattle Center, by Miller/Hull, is a very different earth-sheltered design. This 14,000-square-foot subterranean structure, built of cast-in-place and precast concrete, opens out to the International Fountain and Center Green. On its roof, a paved plaza serves as a forecourt for the adjacent Children's Theater and provides an elevated vantage point on the fountain and the green. This exterior public plaza functions as multiuse event space, effectively doubling the programmable area for the facility. The Fisher Pavilion demonstrates how a building can be subordinated to its context and play a background role yet project a potent architectural presence.

Throughout history, earth-sheltered structures have been some of the best examples of direct, clear, and site-specific architecture.

Soil Remediation

As Arthur Kruckeberg states in *The Natural History of Puget Sound Country*, "Humankind treats soil like dirt."[2] The earth's thin crust is a complex array of living, mutually dependent ecosystems. Fragile yet remarkably resilient, these soils harbor microcosms of miniature life: bacteria, fungi, protozoa, and small invertebrates. As our cities have grown, we have badly mistreated soil, bulldozing it, carting it away to landfills, or paving it over with asphalt and concrete. These actions reflect man's ignorance of soil's role in supporting natural and cultivated vegetation and in filtering water as it flows into aquifers and drainage basins.

Pacific Northwest cities continue to increase in density, and industrial sites are becoming increasingly available for renovation and rehabilitation. Much of the industry that sprawled across the urban environment over the last century has been exported or become outmoded. The Pacific Northwest is experiencing a transformation, from its roots in manufacturing and extractive industry to a more service-end, technology-based economy. This transformation brings with it an opportunity to reclaim the soils within brownfields and Superfund-designated sites as well as rejuvenate the urban environment by incorporating natural processes.

There are several examples of derelict industrial sites that have been redesigned as ecologically sound habitat. The new Seattle Sculpture Park designed by Weiss/Manfredi, New York, transforms a former industrial site along the water's edge into a valuable public green space. The new park creates a cultural edge to the city that highlights the sculpture against the backdrop of Puget Sound and the Olympic Mountains.

The site of Gas Works Park, designed by landscape architect Richard Haag, is a former gasification plant that supplied power to much of Seattle

Seattle Sculpture Park, by Weiss/Manfredi, New York. Photo: Weiss/Manfredi

(Bottom) Gas Works Park, Seattle, by Richard Haag. Photo: Mary Randlett

Stormwater garden at the Water Pollution Control Laboratory, Bureau of Environmental Services, Portland, Oregon, by Miller/Hull with SERA Architects. Photo: Eckert & Eckert

from 1907 to the mid-1950s. A massive soil-cleaning effort was needed to create the famous park that now stands in its place. Portions of the original gasworks remain as powerful sculptures on the shoreline of Lake Union. Recreational park space and public event shelters surround the equipment. Its position on the north shore of the lake, with panoramic views of the downtown skyline, makes it a breathtaking place for sightseeing and enjoying many lakefront activities.

One of the most recent examples of industrial site remediation is the Water Pollution Control Laboratory, located on the Willamette River, in Portland. This project, designed by Miller/Hull with SERA Architects of Portland for the city's Bureau of Environmental Services (BES), expresses the innate beauty of stormwater as an element of landscape form. The bureau is responsible for conducting research on the effect of contaminants on water quality, and the research concept was applied to the site's seven and a half acres of area. The result is an experimental outdoor laboratory that tests how stormwater may be treated in the landscape. Improvements to the former industrial site include stabilizing 900 feet of riverbank soil through bioengineering methods and replacing a collapsed stormwater line that drains a fifty-acre residential and commercial neighborhood situated uphill.

The solution was to create a detention pond and a series of bioswales in which to retain the runoff for a period and allow pollutants to settle out. To do this, landscape architect Robert Murase, the lead site designer on the team, created a one-acre pond formed by two converging circles with a concrete-and-stone flume as the centerpiece of the design. When stormwater pours into the flume, the stones dissipate the water energy and allow solids to settle. The water-borne pollutants—oil and grease, animal waste, pesticides, and heavy metals—are taken up and broken down by the lush plants that encircle the pond. The multitude of bioswales located around the building and integrated into the parking areas makes up a "stormwater garden" that unifies the site approach.

Like the site design, the 40,000-square-foot laboratory is seen as a porous membrane. The ample glazing, screened by a large overhang and steel sunshades, lets in natural light and promotes views of the beautiful river and landscaped ponds. The building, landscape, bioswales, and detention pond are carefully melded with the riverfront so that the city's commitment to environmental quality literally emanates from the site.

FIRE

The sun beats down on the Pacific Northwest through a cover of clouds, and the sky dome glows. The bright overcast sky is ideal for daylighting buildings, reducing energy demands for electrical lighting. Exposure to the direct rays of the sun is less certain in the Pacific Northwest than it is in other climates and at lower latitudes, and residents fervently appreciate and celebrate the sun when it appears.

Alvar Aalto's poignant musings on the roles of sun and light in the Scandinavian climate are equally relevant to the Pacific Northwest:

> Light and sun. Under extreme conditions one can no longer leave the dwelling's access to the sun to chance. Light and air are such important preconditions for living that the haphazard conditions that prevail today must be changed. The norms should . . . require that each dwelling get sun. . . . the sun is a source of energy; but only if we use it in a scientific way. . . . nor can we afford to allow the sun's and the light's energy to remain unused. At the same time we have to eliminate the inconveniences that these factors, under favorable circumstances, can lead to.[3]

Although direct solar energy may be limited in the Pacific Northwest, favorable circumstances for beneficial solar strategies are numerous. First, during winter months, the low-altitude sun ensures a dramatic solar gain to interior spaces. Second, the region's moderate temperatures minimize heat loss to the exterior and reduce demands on thermal mass for solar collection. Third, the moderate climate also lessens the potential for overheating when a building includes large amounts of glazing. And fourth, cloudy conditions favor the natural daylighting of interior spaces without glare, consequently reducing electrical lighting loads, the second-largest consumer of energy (behind natural-gas space heating) in commercial buildings.

Passive Solar

Availability of direct sunshine is not the only factor in establishing the potential for solar energy in a particular location. The geography of the solar position, the temperature ranges, the amount of cloud cover, and the insolation—the total amount of direct, diffuse, and reflected solar radiation that strikes a surface—all contribute to the feasibility of solar architecture.

Northwest sun path at 48 degrees latitude

(Bottom) Percentage of sunshine

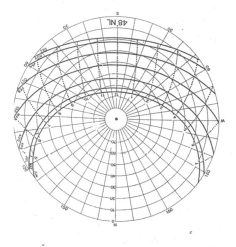

LOCATION	PERCENT OF POSSIBLE SUNSHINE/YEAR
Phoenix	85
Albuquerque	76
Los Angeles	73
Denver	67
Miami	67
Chicago	59
New York	59
Boston	57
Seattle	**45**

LOCATION	AVERAGE DAILY SOLAR ENERGY RECEIVED DURING HEATING SEASON BTU/FT^2–DAY (OCT.–MAR.)	AVERAGE MONTHLY HEATING DUE (BASE 65 DEG. F.) DURING HEATING SEASON (OCT.–MAR.)	SOLAR HEATING INDEX BTU/FT^2–DEG.
Seattle	**560**	**660**	**0.79**
Spokane	660	920	0.72
Boston	680	800	0.85
Chicago	530	880	0.60
Great Falls, MT	770	1000	0.77
Madison, WI	710	1100	0.64
Medford, OR	750	700	1.00

The temperature difference between the outside air and a comfortable indoor environment is less in the Pacific Northwest. In fact, the region has the mildest climate of any place at its latitude in North America. The relatively mild winter temperatures reduce heat loss to the exterior, and less heat is required to raise inside temperatures to a comfortable level. A comparable solar index has been produced by the U.S. Department of Energy, which notes that Seattle and other Pacific Northwest cities have more potential for solar heating than do many other locations in the United States.[4]

Residential architecture and small commercial and public buildings with simple programs are most suitable for passive solar. Homes that utilize natural lighting and ventilation are typical in the Pacific Northwest. This contrasts with the artificial lighting and mechanical ventilation found in office spaces and buildings with complex programs. Office buildings often have significant internal heat gains because of desktop computer equipment, deep plans, and little natural ventilation. In such buildings, the problem is primarily one of cooling and not heating, even in the winter.

In the Pacific Northwest, given the cool temperatures from October through May, heating dwellings is a fundamental consideration. With careful design and use, except at night in the depth of winter, a dwelling can be heated in a sustainable manner, free of charge and without environmental degradation. There are four considerations: (1) collection, (2) storage, (3) distribution, and (4) conservation.

For passive heating, form and layout should maximize timely solar collection. With proper design, residential architecture can be particularly enjoyable at different times of the day or year: east-facing spaces in the morning; west-oriented spaces in the evening; south-facing in winter; and cool spaces in warm weather. At present, clear glazing facing more or less true south (preferably within 20 degrees) is the most effective strategy for passive solar collection. Energy collected from direct-gain solar radiation may be stored directly where it falls, in a wall or a floor, provided the material has a high thermal mass. The darker the material and the higher its thermal capacity, the better its performance.

Both natural and mechanically assisted distribution of captured heat are options in a passive solar structure. In the Pacific Northwest, natural distribution is preferable, with stored heat transmitted by conduction, convection, or radiation. Once the heat has been captured and distributed throughout the structure, the external envelope must lose as little heat as possible. Windows may be double, triple, or "smart" glazed or use glass with special coatings that reflect heat back to internal surfaces. Insulated blinds, curtains, or shutter systems may then be closed at night so as to retain the solar energy captured through glazing during daytime.

Although solar architecture is reasonably feasible in the Pacific Northwest, it may take some time to recoup the financial investment. Extra measures that burden the architectural budget may not make sense in the Pacific Northwest. Passive solar greenhouses, Trombe walls, and active systems such as solar hot water collectors are more appropriate for climates that benefit from extensive solar gain, for example, in the southwestern United States. Direct-gain passive strategies that orient the structure correctly and build in thermal storage mass as an integral part of the building are effective in the Pacific Northwest, in some cases more effective than in sunnier climates, where instantaneous solar gain tends to cause overheating.

Forms generated from this approach that respond to the ambient climate also heighten an occupant's awareness and appreciation of the rhythms of nature and the regenerative cycles of our world. The deployment of seasonal shading devices and operation of movable insulation, which involves decision making on the part of the building's inhabitants, further heightens this awareness.

South-facing glazing captures solar energy on the Greenwood Residence, Galiano Island, British Columbia, by Helliwell + Smith. Photo: Bo Helliwell

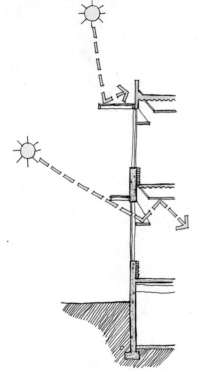

(Top, left) Sunshades on NW Federal Credit Union, Seattle, by Miller/Hull. Photo: Fred Housel

(Top, right) Sunshades on the Water Pollution Control Laboratory, Bureau of Environmental Services. Photo: Eckert & Eckert

Shading diagram of NW Federal Credit Union. Drawing by Alix Henry

Several Pacific Northwest architects have explored the world of passive solar architecture and created some beautiful houses.

Daylighting Techniques
In the Pacific Northwest, daylight is crucial to the quality of a building and the delight one takes in it. Limited access to the sun brings an awareness of its benefits for physical and spiritual health. This spiritual connection with the sun is reflected in the artwork of the Pacific Northwest, from the symbolic carvings of coastal Native peoples to contemporary Northwest School paintings.

In addition to the sun's passive solar energy contributions, properly modulated daylight significantly reduces the need for daytime artificial lighting. Good daylight does not equate with large areas of glazing. The key for a designer is to introduce the correct amount of daylight in a carefully orchestrated manner that supports the planned activities of a given space. Even with the diffused daylight of the Pacific Northwest, plans must address the critical issues of modulating the sun's incidence on a window and controlling the natural light once it enters a space. At certain times of the year, even in temperate climates, excessive solar radiation passing through glazing to interior surfaces causes discomfort.

Properly designed shading elements, or well-placed deciduous plantings, screen out excessive sun in the warm seasons yet admit solar energy when it is beneficial during the cool seasons. Except for buildings with high internal heat loads, the Pacific Northwest has a relatively short period during which cooling is required—generally from July through September. The most effective means of preventing overheating are sunscreens and overhangs (on the south) placed on a building's exterior.

Different types of external shading suit different facade orientations. Permanent, movable, or seasonal shading devices can be used to screen the sun when necessary. The Daylighting Lab, part of the Northwest Energy Alliance—Lighting Design Lab, also provides excellent instruction to students, architects, and owners about controlling daylight on a building's glazed surfaces. Generally, exterior shading elements are horizontal, vertical, or a combination in the "egg-crate" style. Horizontal devices provide the best shading on the south facade when the sun is high in the sky. Vertical shades are effective when the morning sun is low in the east and the afternoon sun is low in the west. Designers in the Pacific Northwest are particularly challenged, given that the solar aspect varies so much over the length of the year (see sun path chart, p. 41).

On Portland's Water Pollution Control Laboratory, designed by Miller/ Hull and SERA Architects, the west glazing captured an excellent view up and down the Willamette River. Although conventional sunscreen design practice called for vertical screens, horizontal steel shading elements suspended approximately four feet off the structure proved 90 percent as effective and still maintained the view.

Because shading devices cut off the view of the sky dome through the windows, they also reduce interior daylight levels. Carefully designed slatted or perforated sunscreens maintain shading while reflecting light into the space. Pacific Northwest architects have designed many excellent solutions that combine effective shading elements with light shelves for interior daylighting. The Central Precinct Police Station in Seattle, by Weinstein/Copeland, and the Northwest Federal Credit Union in Seattle's Northgate area, by Miller/Hull, both utilize steel grates for sunscreens on the south-facing glazing.

Photovoltaic Systems

Photovoltaic cells convert direct sunlight into DC electricity. Although photovoltaics have not been used extensively in the Northwest, they are more widely employed of late owing to the relative first-cost reductions instituted in the last few years. Like any other solar collector, photovoltaics collect more energy when oriented properly. In the Pacific Northwest, with its higher latitude, winter yield is significantly reduced if the cells are not oriented to the south. Photovoltaics are most effective in this region when mounted on sloped roofs close to the angle of the area's latitude plus 15 degrees. Vertical output is also effective, although not nearly as efficient as with a horizontal application.

Photovoltaic arrays may be integrated with a building's structure or skin in several ways. They may be mounted on racks and attached so that they hover over the roof structure. They may be set directly on the roof as a panel system or integrated into the roofing system (i.e., in the form of photovoltaic shingles or standing seam roof panels). They can also be integrated into the skin in the form of other materials, such as spandrel panels, shading devices, or glazing. The new Lillis Business Complex at the University of Oregon, Eugene, by SRG Partnership, Portland, uses photovoltaic cells on the lobby curtain wall both to collect solar energy and to screen the direct gain into the space.

Photovoltaic panels on the Bradner Garden Community Building, Seattle, by SHED. Photo: Scot Carr

(Center and bottom) Lillis Business Complex, University of Oregon, Eugene, by SRG Partnership. Photo: Greg Williams, SRG Partnership

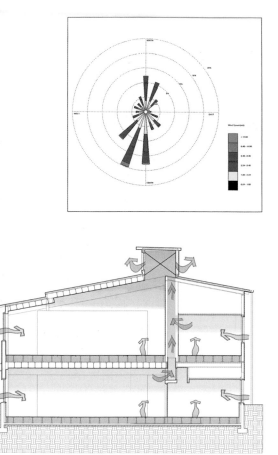

(Top, left) Wind rose diagram

(Top, right) Clackamas High School, Clackamas, Oregon, by BOORA Architects. Photo: Michael Mathas

Ventilation diagram, Wilsonville City Hall, Oregon, by Miller/Hull. Drawing: Miller/Hull

AIR

The flow of air in the Pacific Northwest is heavily influenced by maritime patterns. Warm air moves across the Pacific Ocean, absorbing moisture. Clouds form above the water. Air then travels over the Cascade mountains, rising in elevation, dropping in temperature, and releasing moisture as precipitation. Thus, for much of the year, the Pacific Northwest is cool, humid, and overcast.

As with the sun, the wind may have either a positive or a negative impact on a building's environmental performance. On the positive side, the greatest single advantage is the opportunity for passive cooling through natural ventilation. The Pacific Northwest's relatively cool and temperate climate makes natural ventilation an effective strategy for cooling the interior of buildings.

For good climatic design, one needs to know the wind conditions at a particular site. A designer may consult various environmental agencies such as the Puget Sound Air Pollution Control Agency for wind data. Wind roses also diagram wind frequency and speed for a given time of year.

A building derives maximum benefit from natural ventilation when it is aligned to accept outside air at its high-pressure side and has exhaust points located on the low-pressure side. Wind-direction information for the Pacific Northwest suggests locating intake vents in south to southwest facades and outlets in north facades for most of the year. The larger the outlet size in relation to the inlet size, the higher the velocity of air movement through a space. Air velocity is important, as the occupants' sensation of cooling increases with a more rapid rate of evaporation from their bodies.

In the temperate climate of the Pacific Northwest, wind velocities are frequently low, so a combination of cross-ventilation and stack-ventilation strategies represents a more effective approach. Cross ventilation works in the horizontal dimension, and stack ventilation in the vertical dimension. This involves developing a passive cooling approach in both the plan and the section. Tall rooms, vertical stairways, and atrium spaces with inlet openings at the bottom and exhaust through clerestories at the top are effective air chimneys for natural ventilation.[5]

Thin buildings oriented with their long axes running east-west work best for natural ventilation as well as for daylighting and solar heating, as discussed in this section. Narrow buildings with an open plan or a single loaded-corridor layout are ideal for cross ventilation and stack ventilation. Room configurations and sections in large buildings are often more complex and require innovative ventilation design. When airflow is blocked by an adjacent room or corridor vertical shafts that vent to a clerestory or air chimney, transom vents or relites can transfer air through an adjacent space and facilitate ventilation. Clackamas High School, Oregon, by BOORA Architects, uses operable louvers to provide natural ventilation in each classroom. This project also makes extensive use of daylighting strategies by including sunscreens and light shelves on the south facade.

In the Pacific Northwest, wind conditions at a particular site may be problematic for comfortable outdoor use, but the building's orientation and plan configuration can mitigate excessive wind conditions. Locating outdoor rooms in relation to the combination of sun and wind frequently extends the seasons of outside use. Courtyards often buffer the stronger winds but still capture the breezes that help cool spaces. Many residential and smaller commercial projects employ courtyards in this manner. Paul Kirk (as discussed in chapter 2) was an admirer of the courtyard for its ability to create a positive microclimate, buffer wind, filter summer sun, and offer a human-scale, semi-private refuge for the building's occupants.

The site strategy for a particular structure has a substantial impact on thermal performance and human comfort. In the Pacific Northwest, cold air moving downhill collects at the bottom of valleys and other topographic depressions and creates frost pockets. It is generally preferable to site a building up from the valley floor, with a southerly aspect. If a particular site has a strong prevailing wind condition, a number of natural features may provide shelter. Semipermeable natural landscaping such as hedges, berms, and trees provides effective screens that buffer strong winds into gentle breezes. A slight slope will provide shelter on the lee side without inducing turbulence. A slope of about one in three on the windward side gives the best results. A solid wall provides protection to a distance of four to five times its height. Openings in walls must be carefully planned so that they don't turn into wind funnels. It is advantageous to stagger openings with successive walls or adjacent structures.

WATER

Water is plentiful around the Pacific Northwest during the fall, winter, and spring but scarce throughout the summer. The region is known for cool, drizzly, overcast days, when the surrounding mountains reveal themselves at infrequent and unpredictable intervals. Like the sun, the rain is not heavy, nor is it fleeting, but its gentle omnipresence for much of the year contributes a softness to our senses.

Water, as much as our mountains and forests, defines the Pacific Northwest. This precious resource should be conserved and enhanced with every

Detail of cistern at IslandWood, Bainbridge Island, Washington. ISLANDWOOD and Mithun Architects + Designers + Planners. Photo: Roger Williams

(Left) Bioswale section diagram. Drawing: Alix Henry

(Right) Scuppers send rainwater into bioswale at the Water Pollution Control Laboratory, Bureau of Environmental Services, in Portland, by Miller/Hull. Photo: Eckert & Eckert

building project. Buildings have a serious impact on water ecology. According to the architectural firm Mithun, "The challenge for the future is not a water supply problem, but a water management problem."[6]

At the site and at the building scale, rain is the great equalizer. It falls on roofs, decks and patios, parking lots, and roads. As it strikes these man-made elements, it is transformed into stormwater, which typically is whisked away through gutters, drains, catch basins, and an underground network of storm sewers. The pollutants carried by these systems ultimately degrade the quality of the beautiful waterways that are so plentiful in the Pacific Northwest. The need to mitigate stormwater's destructive potential has given rise to a number of environmental approaches, most aimed at retaining the

water on-site for a period of time. On-site detention and retention strategies with the proper design emphasis express the poetry of water and maximize its innate beauty as a landscape form.

Pacific Northwest environmental agencies have been leaders in establishing design standards for managing stormwater on-site through biofiltration. Bioswales are sunken, planted areas that filter runoff before it enters a storm drain or waterway. Landscape architect Robert Murase has designed several projects in the Portland area that elevate the bioswale to the status of water garden.

Murase's parking lot at the Oregon Museum of Science and Industry features bioswales that combine lush, exuberant wetland grasses with sculpted stonework. This innovative stormwater design, completed in 1996, set a new standard for bioswale design. More recently, Murase collaborated with architects Miller/Hull to produce a design that fully integrates building and site for the Water Pollution Control Laboratory of Portland's Bureau of

Environmental Services. The laboratory building has no gutters; instead, long scuppers extend from the roof, projecting rainwater beyond the building skin and into a rock-lined water garden. (The project's innovative detention pond is discussed in chapter 2.)

Inspired by advances in conservation technology as well as by the rediscovery of traditional systems, Pacific Northwest architects are expressing water's critical environmental role with innovative approaches to architectural form. Roof forms, catchment systems, greenhouse elements containing "living machines," and water conveyance components such as gutters, downspouts, scuppers, and cisterns are all formal architectural elements that express water strategies.

The Flanders Lofts project in Portland, by architects Vallaster and Corl, is an example of how designers can create tectonic expression with rainwater catchment systems. The mid-rise multifamily housing project incorporates a projecting inverted roof form that delivers water to a large downspout, which then irrigates a rooftop garden. The building's structural frame and associated seismic cross-bracing interact with the downspout and its collector head to form a dramatic assembly of building components.

The Newton Library in Surrey, British Columbia, by Patkau Architects, Vancouver, was designed so that the inverted roof gathers natural light into the interior and collects rainwater in a major gutter that runs the length of the building's central axis. The rainwater is then channeled off each end of the building through large galvanized steel scuppers and into rock-filled

catchment areas on grade. From there, it permeates back into the site. This poetic expression of the path of water forms a sculptural ensemble at the building's entry.

Architects, urban designers, and landscape architects working in the Pacific Northwest have unique opportunities to exploit the power and poetry of water. The region's architecture addresses a number of issues, but the relationship between water and buildings is among the most dominant. Not only are there numerous opportunities to express the conservation, detention, retention, and recycling of water within a structure or a site, but there are also many ways in which to express the symbiotic relationship between architecture and water that help articulate the spirit of place.

The Pacific Northwest is home to many fine examples of the poetic use of water to create powerful conceptual architecture. The Weyerhaeuser Headquarters Building in Tacoma, Washington, designed by Skidmore Owings and Merrill's San Francisco office, is a regional architectural icon. It integrates building massing, water feature design, and earth shelter to create a strong conceptual architectural statement, revealing the essence of what Christian Norberg-Schulz calls "natural place."

(Opposite) Scupper at entrance to Newton Library, Surrey, British Columbia, by Patkau Architects. Photo: David Miller

Weyerhaeuser Headquarters Building, Tacoma, Washington, by Skidmore Owings and Merrill. Photo: College of Architecture and Urban Planning

CHAPTER 4

SITE: BUILDING THROUGH ECOLOGICAL PLANNING

CEDAR RIVER WATERSHED EDUCATION CENTER
King County, WA
Jones & Jones Architects and Landscape Architects, Ltd.

VASHON ISLAND TRANSFER AND RECYCLING STATION
King County, WA
The Miller/Hull Partnership

ENVIRONMENTAL SERVICES BUILDING
Pierce County, WA
The Miller/Hull Partnership with Arai Jackson

MAPLE VALLEY LIBRARY
Maple Valley, WA
Johnston Architects with Cutler Anderson Architects

Let us accept the proposition that nature is process, that it is interacting, that it responds to laws, representing values and opportunities for human use with certain limitations and even prohibitions to certain of these. We can take this proposition to confront and resolve many problems.

—Ian McHarg, *Design with Nature*

(Opposite) Visitors center at the Cedar River Watershed Education Center by Jones & Jones Architects and Landscape Architects. Photo: Lara Swimmer

CEDAR RIVER WATERSHED EDUCATION CENTER
King County, WA
Jones & Jones Architects and Landscape Architects, Ltd.

General Description

The Cedar River Watershed receives one and a half times the amount of Seattle's annual rainfall and is the main source for the city's drinking water. The Cedar River Watershed Education Center was created as as result of 1988 legislation to protect the watershed and educate the public about its value as a resource. The Seattle City Council has since designated the watershed an ecological preserve, to be managed for public use, habitat, and water supply. The Rattlesnake Lake recreation area just outside the boundary of the protected watershed was selected as the site for the Watershed Education Center. As a popular recreational area, it required upgrading and environmental repair.

Jones & Jones Architects and Landscape Architects began master planning in 1991. Early goals included siting the education center, programming a new administrative headquarters, and upgrading the park at Rattlesnake Lake. Throughout the design process, the firm viewed the project as an opportunity to reveal hydrological processes to the public, foster appreciation for the source of the city's drinking water, and instill a sense of ecological stewardship. The eco-revelatory theme became the inspiration for the center, which was envisioned as a microcosm of the larger watershed.

The Education Center is a rhythmic arrangement of interior and exterior spaces that encourages movement and invites exploration. Jones & Jones nestled the complex of structures into the site, referencing its historical significance as a railroad route, offering framed views and glimpses of Rattlesnake Ledge and Rattlesnake Lake, and fostering an experience accessible to people of all abilities. The set of buildings clusters around a series of courtyards, generating a dialogue between architecture and landscape. The forest courtyards are receptacles for roof runoff and hold a sequence of inviting, exploratory spaces woven together by a stream and native plants.

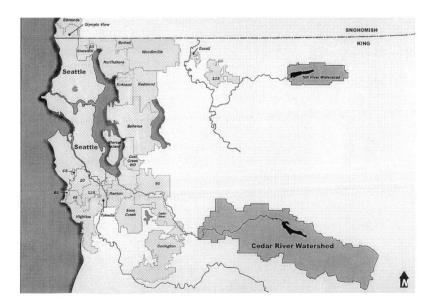

(Opposite) Learning Laboratory building, with view of Rattlesnake Ledge. Photo: Susan Olmsted

Seattle's municipal watersheds. Map: City of Seattle

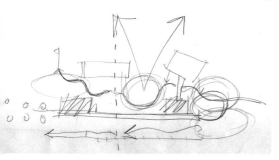

MONCTON WASH.

(Left) Site planning diagram of site and courtyard relationships. Diagram: Nancy Rottle

(Right) Historical photograph of Chicago-Milwaukee Railroad and support station. Photo: City of Seattle Collection

Site History

The Cedar River Watershed has a rich history. Although archaeologists have documented Native American occupation in the upper watershed basin as early as 7400 B.C., railroads and small company towns associated with coal and clay mining produced settlement and industrial impacts beginning in the late 1800s. Logging activity, including two substantial logging camps, followed from the mid-1890s into the 1940s, greatly altering the landscape in the watershed.

The City of Seattle began acquiring land and developing the area as a municipal water source in the early twentieth century, damming the Cedar River in two places to provide water storage in Chester Morse Lake. However, some of the impounded water infiltrated the glacial moraine and reappeared as hillside springs, and in 1916, following construction of the second dam, water filled a valley depression to form Rattlesnake Lake. Rattlesnake Lake became a popular recreational destination, and active use led to substantial degradation of the lake edge and surrounding landscape.

By the mid-1900s, most of the settlements in the watershed had been dismantled in order to protect drinking water quality. By 1996, the City of Seattle had acquired the entire 90,000 acres as the primary source of water for the city and more than two-thirds of King County. For the last ten years, the Seattle city government and the Jones & Jones design team have worked diligently to repair the site. At the same time, they strove to create an unobtrusive vocabulary of intervention within the landscape that aims to foster educational opportunities and encourage environmental stewardship.

The site of the Watershed Education Center was a support station on a railroad line that connected Renton with Milwaukee during the first half of the twentieth century. A settlement of small bungalows housed railroad workers. The legacy of this settlement is a grand allée of native big-leaf maples parallel to the road as well as a compacted site infested with invasive (non-native) plants. The maples and railroad alignment provide an organizing datum, the small building volumes and forms recall the former residential settlement, historic tile artifacts manufactured in the watershed are displayed and used as paving, and thriving watershed plant communities have replaced the invasive landscape.

Climate

The Cedar River Watershed Education Center, located in the forest and mountains between Seattle and Snoqualmie Pass, receives sixty-one inches of rainfall each year. Marine air traveling eastward moves up and over the Cascades; as the air rises, it cools, reducing its capacity to hold moisture and generating significant precipitation. In addition, temperatures at the center are significantly cooler than temperatures in Seattle. This is due to the location's elevation and vegetative cover, as opposed to the concrete and asphalt of Seattle, which has the effect of creating an urban heat island. Rattlesnake Lake also tends to have a positive cooling effect in the summer, as air moves over the water before reaching the center along its shore. Jones & Jones employed simple, low-tech strategies to match the architectural response to local conditions.

Earth Strategies

The master plan and design for the Cedar River Watershed Education Center included restoration of the native landscape. Invasive plants, introduced during the site's use as a railroad support station, had caused extensive damage to the land surrounding the visitors center and along Rattlesnake Lake. Non-native plant species were cleared and replaced with indigenous plant communities that include habitat layers, from moss groundcovers to tree canopies. Although the complete eradication of foreign species has proved challenging, most of the site has been restored. Careful planning and diligent follow-through minimized disturbance to healthy native vegetation during construction.

Site and surrounding Cedar River Watershed basin. Photo: City of Seattle Collection

(Bottom) Project floor plan with associated landscaping. Drawing: Jones & Jones

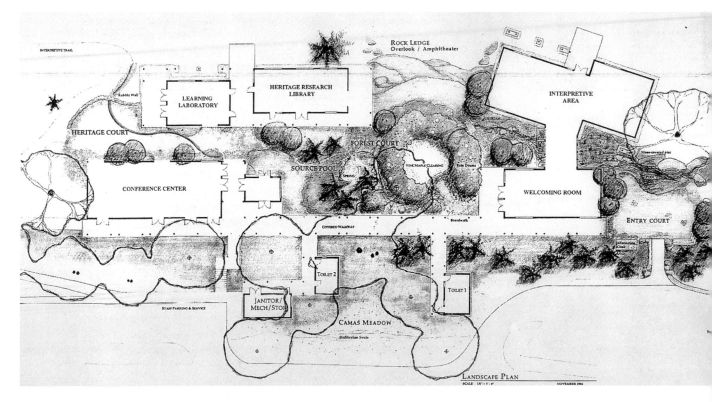

Rattlesnake Lake has been an extremely popular place to picnic, swim, boat, and fish and was in need of infrastructure improvements and environmental restoration. The edge of the lake was deteriorating from poorly delineated parking accommodation and road use. As a solution, Jones & Jones realigned the entrance road and parking areas and restored the park and shoreline with native vegetation, simultaneously benefiting the lake and its users. Soil contamination from former uses was cleaned and mitigated. The new road and parking areas blend gracefully into the landscape, and vehicles no longer barricade the lake edge.

A number of architectural decisions conscientiously consider the earth and its resources. Jones & Jones used component dimensioning to minimize waste from the buildings at the visitors center. Green roofs on some of the structures blend into the environment, reduce runoff, and help insulate the interior spaces underneath (some of the green roofs cover exterior walkways, and others cover restrooms). The architecture utilizes natural and recycled materials including 98 percent FSC-certified wood, recycled-wood flooring, minimally processed materials, water-based clear finishes, and fly-ash-component concrete slabs and outdoor terraces. Jones & Jones looked far into the future and designed the buildings so that they could all be disassembled, moved, and reassembled elsewhere later.

Fire Strategies

Although the architects examined multiple strategies for both heating and cooling the buildings, the design team found that the most basic solutions were best suited to the situation. The heating system relies on good-quality residential-scale heat pumps with economizers for greater efficiency. The buildings are exceptionally well insulated, so supplied heat is maintained longer. Insulated headers and rigid insulation above the exposed roof framing eliminate thermal bridging. Walls are well insulated also, and windows filled with argon gas minimize heat loss. Daylight enters the interior spaces through generous wood-framed side windows, positioned both high and low for an even balance of light. Deep overhangs provide shade, and trees become light fixtures as they filter the direct rays of the sun and glow with dappled light.

Air Strategies

Nights at the Cedar River Watershed are always cool, and daytime air moves across water and through vegetation before reaching the center. The ventilation strategy capitalizes on the availability of fresh cool air. Operable double-hung windows provide natural cross ventilation, and generous overhangs protect against overheating in summer. The deep overhangs also create cool, sheltered spaces for mingling outside the buildings.

Water Strategies

One of the primary goals of the Watershed Education Center is to teach visitors about water and human interactions with it. A series of transitional spaces throughout the center allows a variety of relationships with water and nature, from completely exposed, to semi-sheltered, to enclosed. Water is revealed as an artistic element, a playful and interactive component that animates each space. Movement through the site enables the visitor to experience the watershed in microcosm. A stream greets visitors as they ar-

(Top, left) Forest courtyard layers land-scape and built forms. Photo: Nancy Rottle

(Below, left) Entrance path follows the course of the stream. Photo: Susan Olmsted

(Top, right) Designed for disassembly. Photo: Susan Olmsted

rive. Following the stream to its source leads them through artful demonstrations that quietly teach about interconnectedness—the water cycle and how humans have interacted with patterns of water within the watershed. The sounds and rhythms of water create an engaging journey.

The education center has three sources of water. The first is a well that supplies potable water. The second source, the Cedar River, supplies nonpotable water for the fire suppression system and irrigation. Huge penstocks siphon water from upstream (the same penstocks that pull water for the City of Seattle), which is then diverted to the fire suppression system. The nonpotable system requires continuous flushing, so the water flows through it, and then through the center's stream and down to Rattlesnake Lake, where it rejoins the river through the groundwater. This detour models the pattern and flow of streams in the watershed, a beneficial scenario. The third source of water is precipitation, and a variety of strategies address the path of this water as it moves from the sky to the earth. Two types of roofs intercept water as it falls from the sky. Green roofs, the first type, absorb much of the precipitation directly and support raised parcels of habitat for birds, insects, and plant communities. Steeply sloped metal roofs, the second type, direct water through carefully designed gutters and downspouts, which channel it into the stream, artful catchment basins, and a series of bioswales and

(Opposite) Green roof blends into the restored landscape. Photo: Nancy Rottle

(Preceding page, top) Transparency is highlighted at night. Windows have operable double-hung sashes. Photo: Lara Swimmer

(Preceding page, bottom) Layers of refuge: Exposed, semi-sheltered, and enclosed. Photo: Susan Olmsted

(Right) Axis of covered walkway focuses on allée of maples. Photo: Lara Swimmer

(Bottom) Buildings cluster around a forest courtyard where public art enhances the sight and sound of water. Photo: Lara Swimmer

The Cedar River Watershed Education
Center offers an unobtrusive fore-
ground to Rattlesnake Ledge. Photo:
Lara Swimmer

infiltration basins. Pollutants from the road and parking area are treated in a chain of bioswales that release clean water back to the earth. Sand-set paving, where possible, further reduces runoff, increasing the opportunity for groundwater replenishment. With the exception of a demonstration area that includes a home-scale rain barrel for rainwater harvesting, water is not collected and stored on-site, since it is abundantly available year-round.

Postscript
An ecological project requires a change in our way of thinking about de-sign, implementation, and ongoing operations and maintenance. Planning for the Cedar River Watershed Education Center began well before the concept of sustainability was widespread. In this sense, the center embraces sustainable strategies to a remarkable degree. Along the way, Jones & Jones, a firm long noted for its commitment to working within the earth's capacity to renew itself, educated the client, the contractors, the staff, and now the public about opportunities for reducing our impact on natural resources and, moreover, on becoming stewards of the environment.

While the Watershed Education Center deftly illustrates a myriad of strategies that we can all use to conserve resources, perhaps a few areas

Downspouts serve as an artistic element in the courtyard. Photo: Nancy Rottle

could have been pushed further during the design phase, given a different political construct or a more flexible budget. Passive (solar) strategies and ground-source heat, initially suggested by the design team, were rejected early on, because the systems and methods were unconventional, costly, and at the time viewed as tangential to the focused interpretive mission of the center. The simple, familiar technology of residential construction seemed the best fit for a project that was meant to resonate with homeowners and demonstrate strategies that people could apply in their daily lives.

During the construction phase, contractors needed to understand the intent of the project and adjust their accustomed patterns of work. Tree protection, green materials, and component dimensioning all minimized the project's resource impact. Though straightforward, these strategies were not standard practice, and proper implementation required good communication by all team members. This level of design team attention carried through to the essential details that reinforced the eco-friendly theme.

The Heritage Courtyard provides an informal space for educational activities and demonstrations. Photo: City of Seattle

Interconnections between the buildings and the exterior courtyards were integral to the success of the design; for example, gutters and downspouts that displayed the path of water from the roof to the earth were key aspects. Considered within the context of the whole project, the slope of a gutter is normally a minor detail, but to effectively display the flow of water it required special attention at all levels for successful implementation throughout the project.

Once built, a project emphasizing ecology requires stewardship. Standard maintenance and operations practices are often somewhat at odds with the larger goals of a sustainable project. The forest ecosystem of the watershed, for example, requires a different type of maintenance than does a typical urban park. Education efforts continue to include maintenance personnel and staff members, who soon embrace the sustainable strategies and systems.

Inherent to sustainability is the idea of interconnectedness in both built and natural systems, from the smallest details to the whole. Each component of a project affects the others, just as the project itself affects the world around it. The Cedar River Watershed Education Center shows that the ongoing success of a sustainable project hinges upon good communication and judicious education at every level, from inception to occupation and continuing stewardship.

VASHON ISLAND TRANSFER AND RECYCLING STATION
King County, Washington
Thomas/Wright, Inc. and the Miller/Hull Partnership

General Description
In June 1999, the Vashon Island Landfill reached capacity and terminated operations. Following the closure of the landfill, the Vashon Island Transfer and Recycling Station began accepting solid waste and recyclables for transfer off the island. Thomas/Wright, Inc., prime consultants and lead engineers, with The Miller/Hull Partnership as a subconsultant, was hired to design the new transfer facility. The client and consultant team recognized the project as an opportunity to display the potential for waste-stream reduction. Paladino & Company, a sustainability consultant, reviewed the design and specifications and made recommendations for maximizing resource efficiency.

The project's major goals were to emphasize the usefulness of recycled materials and to stretch the limits on incorporating recycled-content materials in building construction. The design team envisioned a composition of structure, cladding, and art that would engage the public and encourage recycling. The King County Arts Commission component, an interactive concrete wall with holes through which participants throw recyclables, became an important educational opportunity.

Today, the Vashon Island Transfer and Recycling Station stands as a cadent integration of materials, form, landscape, program, and ideology. It illustrates how a utilitarian building can be both functional and elegant.

Community
The Vashon Island community was heavily involved in the development of this civic structure. A citizens' advisory committee reviewed the project during the design process. It recommended and gained approval from the

(Opposite) Overall view of Vashon Island Transfer and Recycling Station, with scale house in foreground. Photo: Fred Housel

(Left) Detail of recycling deposit. Photo: Fred Housel

(Right) Trucks load under the shed form. Photo: Sian Roberts

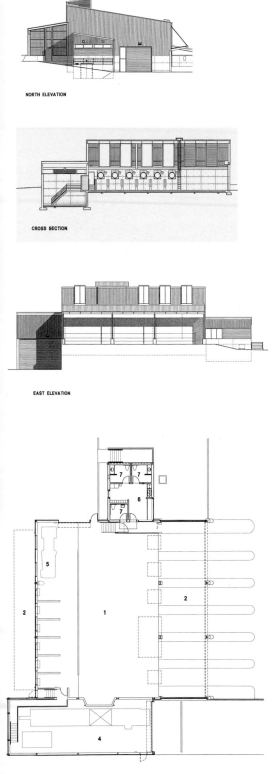

NORTH ELEVATION

CROSS SECTION

EAST ELEVATION

County Arts Commission to utilize the public art budget for the project. These funds were earmarked for a more "conventional" public building. Two groups, a work release program run by the King County Facilities and Maintenance Division and the Chronic Inebriants Program, grew and installed all of the plant material for the landscaping.

Site

Miller/Hull was involved in the site selection process from the inception of the project. After community participation, environmental consideration, and careful analysis of circulation patterns, the parcel adjacent to the existing landfill was selected. To ameliorate possible detrimental effects to nearby residents, the design team utilized earth berms to conceal the sight and noise of the fire and water tanks.

Site planning and circulation patterns drove the project, and the design team created an experience out of the functional sequence of events required by the transfer station. As in the recycling process, a series of paths sort traffic, people, and materials into organized flow sequences. The building shifts scales in response to the different paths of people and vehicles, introducing a sheltering canopy and artwork where people walk to toss their recyclables into bins through holes in the concrete wall.

Earth Strategies

New construction accounts for a large percentage of resource consumption worldwide. Recycling materials, both during construction and as a function of the building, reduces the strain on the earth's resources.

The following recycled materials and strategies are incorporated in the Vashon Island Recycling and Transfer Station:

- Recycled material was used as a sub-base for road beds.
- In general, heavy steel sections (wide flange, tube steel, and angles) contain up to 90 percent recycled steel. Light-gauge steel sections (metal studs and siding) contain 15–35 percent recycled steel. The roof and wall structures, roofing, and siding of the transfer building and scale house are all made of steel.
- Concrete contained a minimum of 10 percent fly ash in the cementitious material.
- Ceramic tiles in restrooms contain a minimum of 50 percent domestically recycled glass.
- Rubber flooring in staff work areas has a minimum of 50 percent recycled content.
- Mineral wool insulation is made from iron ore blast-furnace slag, with postindustrial recycled content of 75 percent.
- Gypsum wallboard (GWB) has a minimum of 8–10 percent recycled-content gypsum and exterior gypsum sheathing with 100 percent recycled-content paper backing.
- Interior paint is of recycled-content.

Sustainable materials and solutions include:

- Low-E glass for windows, doors, and clerestories.
- Natural cork tackboard in meeting room and offices.

- Formaldehyde-free MDF cabinet substrate.
- Low-VOC form release product.
- Landscape berm and sound wall, which minimize noise pollution.
- Shielded light fixtures, which minimize light pollution.

Fire Strategies

Large, translucent windows supply daylight to the transfer station. The steel framing and cladding, painted white, helps reflect and distribute the available daylight throughout the space. Low-E glass prevents excess heat gain from the administrative offices and scale-house windows, thereby reducing cooling loads.

Water Strategies

The existing landfill, which contained serious contaminants harmful to both humans and the local environment, was covered by an impermeable cap. This prevented leaching of potentially harmful waste into the groundwater. In order to conserve the island's water resources, the landscape design utilized plant material that does not require irrigation.

(Opposite, top) North elevation (top), cross section (middle), east elevation (bottom). Drawing: Miller/Hull

(Opposite, bottom) Building plan. Drawing: Miller/Hull

Interior of main transfer station space. Photo: Fred Housel

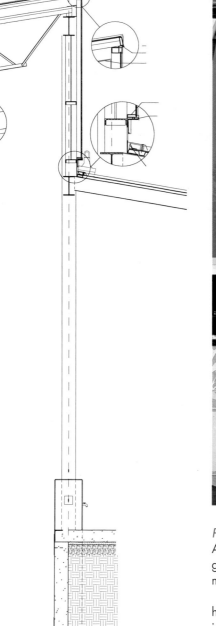

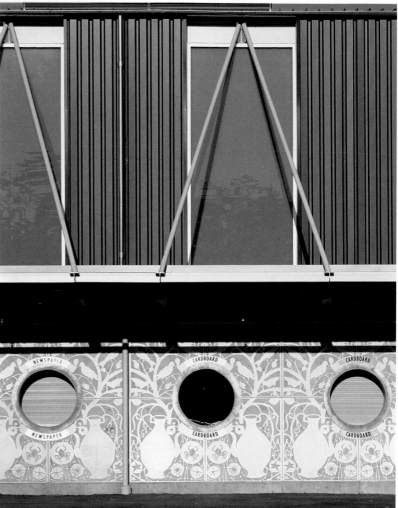

(Left) Building wall section shows
translucent panel system at clerestory.
Drawing: Miller/Hull

(Right) Recycling bays with projecting
canopies. Photo: Fred Housel

Postscript

Although the facility engaged many sustainable-design elements and strategies, particularly for a project of its type, a few shortcomings should be mentioned.

As a transfer station and recycling facility, this project ideally should have optimized construction-waste recycling. However, the site was on an island and adjacent to an existing landfill, and the cost of hauling the waste off the island for recycling was significant compared to the alternative of depositing the waste next door.

There was no septic system at this site, and the wastewater used to wash down the pit is considered leachate and was piped to the landfill. A drainfield was installed to handle the three toilets on the property. The use of composting toilets could have eliminated the need to install the septic system, but the project clients were reluctant to ask their staff to use this unfamiliar type of toilet.

The public art piece, an exterior mural designed to highlight recycling, included labels indicating which recyclable material was supposed to be

Overview of facility from the south. Photo: Fred Housel

(Bottom) The north elevation bridges the upper public level and the lower service level. Photo: Fred Housel

thrown through each hole, but bins behind the holes were assigned to different materials almost immediately. The facility operators placed handwritten cardboard signs over the artwork to show people where to dump their recyclables. In hindsight, the design would have been more sustainable if the signage had been planned to accommodate future changes.

ENVIRONMENTAL SERVICES BUILDING
Pierce County, Washington
The Miller/Hull Partnership with Arai Jackson

General Description

In 1992, Pierce County acquired more than 700 acres of land from Lone Star Northwest for expansion of its adjacent wastewater treatment plant. Steilacoom-grade gravel, a standard for public works projects throughout Washington, had been mined from this pit for more than 100 years. As a result, the pit and the smaller, adjoining county gravel pit were completely barren, devoid of all vegetation and soil.

As part of Arai Jackson's overall master plan to reclaim our resources, the Environmental Services Building (ESB) was intended to house Pierce County's Environmental Services Division, which includes Stormwater Management, Solid Waste, Water Programs, Wastewater, and Public Outreach. Designed by The Miller/Hull Partnership, it is the first county building on the site, a 50,000-square-foot structure housing offices, meeting spaces, and public interpretive exhibits. This first-phase building and its associated site improvements set the standard for future development throughout the 928 acres.

The ESB is a rhythmic arrangement of solid support cores and open office spans. The coupling of open spaces with support cores provides access to daylight and fresh air for each employee along with programmatic support spaces such as copying and storage. The offset patterning of the cores contributes to a sense of permeability, linking interior spaces to both eastern and western exterior expanses.

Site

The dramatic site for the Environmental Services Building is on a plateau overlooking the gravel mine and the surrounding bluffs that slip into Puget Sound. The orientation of the building acknowledges the eastern view of the Sound, while the site aligns with the axis connecting Mount Olympus and Mount Rainier. The open siting and orientation of the building allow ample access to sunlight and fresh air. Although the siting is north-south, rather than the environmentally optimum east-west, the architectural devices used to offset this condition are important parts of the structure's overall vocabulary. The deep overhangs on the eastern and western faces of the building help prevent direct sun penetration for most of the workday yet preserve the regional views that foster a distinct sense of place. The availability of southern sunlight is an important component of the integrated strategy for heating, cooling, and lighting, and the prevailing wind patterns from the southwest offer options for natural ventilation.

Earth Strategies

The concrete expression recalls the site's history and becomes the defining architectural and integration strategy.

Office pods, or concrete "chimneys," serve as the primary structure for the building. This provides a programmatic benefit, since it allows the office bays to remain column-free. The chimneys also offer a mechanical benefit, acting as a thermal mass that absorbs heat during the day and then radiates it at night while the building is flushed. Cool outside air circulates though the building at night, discharging heat and precooling the concrete

for the next day. Plants at the base of the chimneys help clean the air and offer a psychological connection to the earth, while views to the exterior are no more than thirty-five feet away from every workstation.

The building features inventive uses of recycled and renewable materials throughout, and a public atrium provides space for educational displays highlighting the sustainable features of the project.

(Top, left) Site plan diagrams climate conditions. Drawing: Miller/Hull

(Bottom, left) West facade of main office block, with deep overhang for solar control. Photo: Eckert & Eckert

(Top, right) Floor plan diagram of main level. Drawing: Miller/Hull

(Bottom, right) Concrete mass of structure precools building for the next day. Photo: Eckert & Eckert

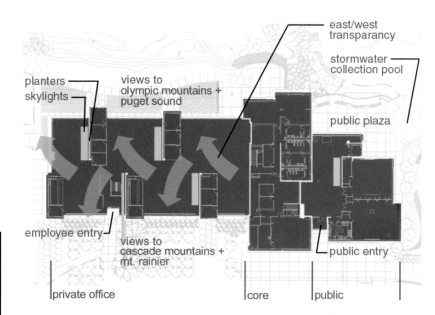

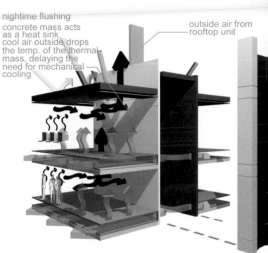

nightime flushing
concrete mass acts
as a heat sink
cool air outside drops
the temp. of the thermal
mass, delaying the
need for mechanical
cooling

outside air from
rooftop unit

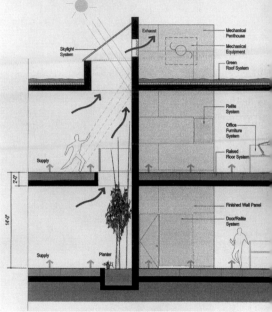

Fire Strategies

The chimneys are oriented to maximize southern exposure. Sunlight enters through the glass at the top of the pod, radiating heat that is absorbed by the concrete and generating a temperature differential between the top and the base of the chimney. The differential produces a stack effect, whereby ventilation is accelerated as heat rises up and out. This reduces the building's mechanical requirements and saves energy.

The openings at the top of the chimneys also admit daylight, providing significant savings by meeting lighting needs with fewer electric lights. The thin building footprint and open office arrangement follow the European standard; every work space is within thirty-five feet of an exterior window and the accompanying daylight.

Air Strategies

Air is supplied through a raised floor plenum, offering occupants individual control over their immediate environment. Air delivered through the floor can be supplied at a more moderate temperature and lower velocity compared to forced-air systems, and exhaust air and fresh air do not mix, which means air quality is better than that provided by conventional systems. Cool

(Top, left) Interior at chimney base. Photo: Eckert & Eckert

(Top, right) Mechanical system diagram. Drawing: Miller/Hull

(Bottom, right) Section shows thermal chimney system design. Drawing: Miller/Hull

air enters low, moves past occupants at low speed, and then rises up and out through the chimneys as it heats up.

Occupants also maintain control over their immediate environment with operable windows. During the swing seasons, the mechanical system can be turned off, and east- and west-facing windows may be opened to gain additional fresh-air circulation.

Water Strategies

Stormwater is brought to the surface and treated as an interpretive opportunity. Rainwater drops from roof scuppers into a series of ponds and then enters a bioswale, where it is treated before it reaches the infiltration pond. Along the route, a flow splitter incorporated in a public plaza routes stormwater along three distinct paths in order to demonstrate the effectiveness of different stormwater management strategies.

Drought-tolerant and indigenous plant material has been installed throughout the site. Irrigation is incorporated at the playfields and other landscaped areas, mainly for initial plant establishment. The irrigation system is equipped with rain gauges and overrides the automatic timer when irrigation is not needed. Once plants are established, irrigation will be minimized.

(Opposite, top) Stairs at chimney base. Photo: Eckert & Eckert

(Opposite, bottom) Scuppers deliver rainwater to detention ponds. Photo: Eckert & Eckert

Wooden public walkway passes over detention pond. Photo: Eckert & Eckert

MAPLE VALLEY LIBRARY
Maple Valley, Washington
Johnston Architects with Cutler Anderson Architects

General Description
The Maple Valley Library is nestled into a thick second-growth forest, recall-ing the original landscape that gave the town its name. The building had a small budget but large goals regarding the design. It aimed to meet the community's long-term needs while preserving the essence of its past. The architects asked several major questions at the outset. The first was, "Why not put the library in the developed area of the town and preserve this forest?" The second was, "If you insist on putting the library here, can we limit parking to what is required by code and promote alternative means of transportation?" The third was, "Will the city of Maple Valley accept an innovative approach to stormwater management?" The answers all sup-ported the design solution that evolved. A series of parallel programmatic questions allowed the designers to mold their response to the constraints of the densely treed site and topography.

Earth Strategies
Approached from a busy arterial road, the library is barely visible through the trees. In the parking area, the site darkens in the shadows of the tall trees that have been carefully preserved on the site's one and three-quarter acres. The parking lot is based on an arborist's plan and comprises a series of clustered spaces nestled within the looming Douglas fir, western red ce-dar, hemlock, and scattered vine maple. The building is similarly tucked into the forest, with the low part of the shed roof and the patrons' entrance on

(Opposite) Dappled natural light filters through forest outside children's read-ing room at the Maple Valley Library. Photo: Art Grice

Entrance porch is a transition space between inside and outside. Photo: Art Grice

(Bottom) Windows wrap corners to gather light. Photo: Art Grice

(Top) West elevation sketch includes public entry and courtyard. Drawing: James Cutler

(Bottom) East elevation is tall, buffering the busy arterial. Drawing: James Cutler

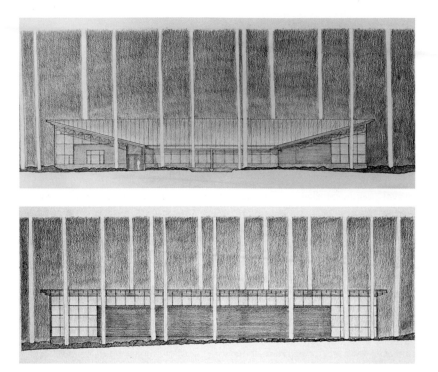

the forest side. This minimal facade, a combination of cedar shingles and abundant glass, recedes into the forest. From the interior of the library, the forest seems to enter the building through these large windows, blurring the boundary between inside and outside. The transition space from exterior to interior is a modest covered entry. Slim columns meet a stem wall of cast-in-place concrete that wraps around the entire building. The rhythmic, slender structure of the library is evident on the inside and the outside and mimics the surrounding forest.

The designer's decisions regarding the form and detailing of the library result in efficient use of materials. The building is a simple, rectilinear U-shape plan with a shed roof. The form permits a repetitive structural configuration built with off-the-shelf steel-and-wood trusses, resulting in straightforward details. While it minimizes material waste, it also adds to the flexibility of the interior spaces; they are open and unobstructed. The central reading room is an expansive space of exposed structural steel and wood members where the books take center stage. The material palette reveals the essential components of the building without superfluous adornment. CDX plywood remains exposed on the exterior soffits. The interior finishes are similarly unadorned, missing the typical GWB sheathing. The result is a graceful, serene public space that is also quite functional.

Fire Strategies

The conjunction of heavy tree coverage, frequently overcast climate, and valley location results in the need to maximize the amount of natural light that enters the library. Sunshades were not necessary because of the orientation of the building, deep overhangs, and the dense trees, which keep out most direct sunlight. Filtered light enters through the clerestory windows on the east and the tall window walls that compose the northeast and southeast corners. Dappled light graces the interior of the library and dissolves the building into the landscape. The courtyard walls are principally glass, even though they face the west. Because the site is thickly treed, the building's design is free from some constraints typically imposed on more exposed sites.

Water Strategies

The roof sheds to the forest side of the building, directing all rainwater to a single, dramatic open downspout designed to accommodate up to 300 gallons of water a minute. Rain travels from metal roof to gutter to downspout and into this pool in the central courtyard, where it percolates through the gravel bottom for filtering. The courtyard is a sculptural pool formed with small concrete steps designed to catch organic debris in order to facilitate a moss garden. The design is a poetic demonstration of roof runoff, linking the building to its elements and the patrons to the local weather.

Postscript

The gutters are slightly undersized and so do not work quite as well as intended. Reduced function occurs only with extremely heavy rainfall, when water overflows the gutters. But because the perimeter contains only natural vegetation and absorbent forest duff, the issue is minor. The soil absorbs all of the water that comes off the nearly 10,500-square-foot roof. The architects considered the organic debris from the trees as part of the equation when planning the rainwater management system. They indicated to the

Continuous clerestory glazing floats the roof plane. Photo: Art Grice

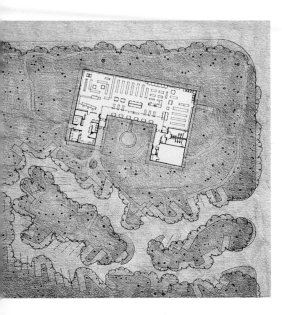

Site plan shows building and parking areas set in forest. Drawing: James Cutler

client that the roof would require extra attention because of the fall of needles and branches, and the client accepted this need as a reasonable trade-off. Forest-generated debris has been less than what would be experienced in a decimated forest. Maintaining the existing canopy has preserved the building's ability to withstand extreme weather and decreased the impact of debris, heat gain, and interior glare.

The exposed, common materials are holding up very well in general; however, the wood members of the roof trusses that are carried to the outside of both ends of the U are showing weathering. But with the necessary protection, the use of these materials, which are readily recognized as products of the surrounding forest, becomes less of a risk. The degradation they suffer, such as discoloration and children's writing on the wooden sills, is more an indication of the nature of the materials. The architects believe this weathering reinforces their goal of connecting buildings with their roots and surroundings.

The site design is one of the most successful aspects of the project. The building embraces the existing second-growth forest, and parking is integrated into the site in an unobtrusive manner. The building is positioned to allow light in but protect books and people from heat, glare, and traffic noise. The successful site design was born out of an early meeting between the clients and architects, which took place in the forest. Upon leaving their cars, the group experienced the 90-degree summer heat. Twenty feet into the forest, the temperature dropped by 10 degrees and bird sounds replaced traffic noise. There were huckleberries to snack on. Architect Ray Johnston asserts, "It was a wonderful event, discussing what to do with the library and parking while sitting in a very special place. I think that, through extremely attentive site and building design, we have preserved the qualities that we experienced that day."

The interior spaces in the library merge with the preserved forest on the exterior. A nursing log was repositioned so it could be viewed from the more intimate seating near the entry, while the children's area shares the canopy of a large vine maple, and a cedar grove surrounds the adult lounge. Each space elucidates the continuity between the exposed natural materials on the inside and their sources on the outside. The filtered sunlight on the inside of the library wonderfully maintains the quality of light experienced by the design team and architects during their initial meeting in the forest.

Informed and educated design decisions contribute to the success of attentive site and building design. The architects read studies on relocating forest duff to act as a biofilter for parking area runoff. Maple Valley building officials cooperated by allowing the proposal to be tested on the library, even though the approach was not part of the county water-quality manual.

There has been remarkable positive feedback on the design. Johnston mentions a telling encounter with a Friends of the Library board member at the library's opening ceremony. He explains that early in the design process, she had wanted a library with a "classical look with Doric columns, etc." At the opening ceremony, she "thanked us for providing a building that had all the power and presence she had hoped within an aesthetic that expressed the identity of Maple Valley."

Drainage detail at downspout and sculptural stepped pool. Photo: Art Grice

CHAPTER 5

LIGHT CONSTRUCTION: RESOURCE-CONSERVING BUILDING

BRADNER GARDEN COMMUNITY BUILDING
Seattle, WA
SHED

MATERIALS TESTING FACILITY
Vancouver, BC
Busby + Associates Architects

PETITE MAISON DE WEEKEND REVISITED
Patkau Architects

The building accommodates processes but is in itself a process, and both circumstances call for the presence of energy. Thus energy is installed in the heart of architecture in two ways: through the energy consumption of buildings (or more accurately, of the building's users) in thermal regulation, water heating, lighting, etc., and through the energy needed to organize, modify and repair the built domain. In other words: through the energy consumed by the process that the building houses, and through the energy consumed by the process that the building itself is. We shall call the former an energy of maintenance, and the latter an energy of construction.
—Luis Fernández-Galiano, *Fire and Memory: On Architecture and Energy*

(Opposite) The butterfly roof and windmill at the Bradner Garden Community Building work together to harvest rainwater for the gardens. Photo: David Miller

BRADNER GARDEN COMMUNITY BUILDING
Seattle, Washington
SHED

General Description

Bradner Garden is a city-owned park, organized and operated by the community. It consists of demonstration gardens, P-patches, and a basketball court. The program for this project calls for the adaptation of an existing concrete-block structure and provision of a public restroom, kitchen, tool storage area, community meeting room, and horticultural resource center. The design aims to address all user groups with a building that is environmentally responsive and responsible and harvests resources available on-site. In this design, the concrete masonry building is renovated to accommodate unconditioned space including a restroom, kitchen, and storage area. A newly constructed, conditioned community space is located next to the modified building. The two spaces are joined under a single butterfly roof that shelters the structures while harvesting water and solar energy. The flexible, covered space between the buildings creates a protected passage with a hand-washing sink and drinking fountain and space for community information exchange.

Earth Strategies

The building site shaped the initial design considerations for the project. An unarticulated, no-frills CMU structure with a low, sloped gable roof sat on the site. Its modification became the first design challenge when the architect considered how to reuse the existing building to advantage without allowing it to limit the design. The project proposes an integrated exploration of environmental strategies through a responsive and environmentally regenerative architecture. At its core is restoration and regeneration of the site.

In addition to the site-scale environmental strategies, the project integrates many environmentally considered materials such as lumber containing

(Opposite) Dusk view of Bradner Garden Community Building. Photo: Scot Carr

(Left) Conceptual model of the butterfly roof, which collects both water and energy. Photo: Scot Carr

(Right) Conceptual sketch shows use of natural lighting in the community meeting room. Drawing: Scot Carr

The existing CMU structure was modified and incorporated into the new building. Photo: Scot Carr

(Right) Skylights admit light into the meeting room. Photo: Scot Carr

(Opposite, top, right) Solar panels were integrated into the roof design. Photo: Scot Carr

(Opposite, bottom, right) Large operable door and operable windows create cross ventilation. Photo: Scot Carr

locally recycled plastic, FSC-certified lumber and finish materials, and low-VOC coating. The meeting room interior finish is Dakota Burl, made from an agricultural by-product, sunflower hulls.

Fire Strategies
With the goal of creating an environmentally regenerative architecture, the design explores methods for giving back, not just breaking even. The butterfly roof is a graphic representation of this approach; it is a collector. The roof is designed to integrate the largest array of photovoltaic panels in Seattle, 8.8kW. Currently, forty 130-watt panels (5.3kW) are mounted on the roof with simple, inexpensive detailing; the lower cost allowed for a larger solar array.

The resulting design is a clean integration of the structural and electrical systems, easy to build and maintain yet adding to the overall aesthetic of the project. With these panels, the building is a net energy producer, generating more power than it uses and supplying energy to the community via its connection to the utility grid. When the building produces more power than it uses, the electric meter runs backward. The system is deliberately oversized for the building's electrical needs. The form of the roof orients the panels to collect the most energy during peak demand times, in the morning and the afternoon.

Daylight infuses the interior spaces, reducing electrical demand inside the buildings. A large skylight in the public restroom eliminates the need for electrical light during the day. Windows and skylights wash the community room in warm daylight. Light bounces in through low, slight windows at floor level and gleams through substantial openings high up and in the roof.

Air Strategies

The windows and skylights are operable and supply adequate cross ventilation to the meeting room, the only conditioned space of the project. There is no mechanical cooling system in this building. A large door on the south facade opens up to augment airflow. The building has been well insulated, and a small gas fireplace is the only supplemental heat source. During cold months, it is set to maintain a 50-degree interior temperature during those times when the building is not in use. When the building is in use, the thermostat can be set to a more comfortable temperature.

The CMU structure is thought of as the project's utilitarian, agricultural shed. It is entirely unconditioned space, designed with the objective of seeking the minimal solution for the needs of the project. As a result, the vertical structural members remain exposed. Horizontal members made of recycled-plastic lumber span the space between the vertical structure to create a secured, but outdoor, room for storing tools. The restroom is also within this open area, carefully conceived as open enough to be comfortable for a

(Bottom, left) Conceptual sketch of solar panel–covered roof. Drawing: Scot Carr

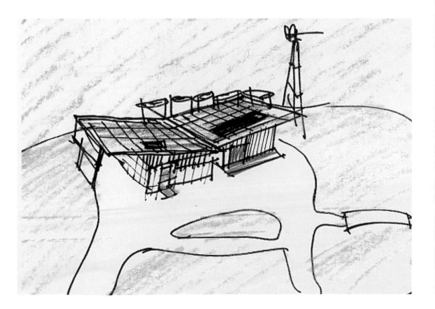

little while (because it is not secluded and unsafe) but not comfortable enough to encourage lengthier stays (because it is not hidden and unnoticed).

Water Strategies

The large roof covering the structures is configured to collect and divert more than 30,000 gallons of rainwater to three 2,500-gallon galvanized water tanks. These tanks hold water for uses around the building, such as washing tools, watering plants, and composting. The catchwater element is intended to be gravity fed. Overflow from the tanks travels to a pond, where the windmill pumps it along for use on higher parts of the site. The architecture is expressive about this catchwater system. The roof reaches dramatically into the sky through the butterfly form that drains water to the central gutter. The gutter is a spine that marks the community gathering place, on the axis with the garden and the building.

Postscript

Although the building was designed with an extensive water collection and storage system, funding for these elements has not been provided. To date, this aspect of the project is unfinished, a concern to the architect, who views it as essential to the building and a lost potential. There are lessons to be considered in the open screen above the CMU building that houses the restroom and tool storage space. The openness is leading to problems with vandals, rain, and wind. In order to address these concerns, the architect is examining design modifications, observing that the idea for the screen might have been developed too literally to be functional in this setting. New materials were tested on this structure, providing insight into materials

Conceptual sketch of gutter spine from below. Drawing: Scot Carr

(Bottom) View of the modified CMU structure. Photo: Scot Carr

considered sustainable. Dakota Burl was used as an interior wall finish. It is available in four-by-eight-foot sheets, and, per an early design decision, it was ripped into six-inch strips that would overlap, making the system easy to build and replace because it is self-trimming and at a manageable scale. The material is sealed on all sides and nailed at twelve inches on center, but installation has revealed that the product moves significantly and bows in places.

Among the project's successes is the implementation of architectural strategies appropriate for a community building; it has been designed to accommodate the hands of the community. They have a unique connection to the structure, as the budget included construction of the shell and community members were accountable for finishing aspects of the building and making the components useful. The architect designed the restroom with backer board, which was installed by the contractor, and the final mosaics were completed by the community.

Community members were also responsible for building the tool racks, bulletin boards, and signage. The building engages the community through hard construction work and activates interest in sustainable strategies through unconcealed systems. Hear the wind generator spinning. Look at rain traveling down the sloped roof to the central gutter. Visitors enjoy watching the power meter spin backward; people have commented that they often go to look at the meter just to see what is happening.

The success of this project lies in the integration of sustainable strategies with the architecture; design is not separated from its function. As a result, the users of the building are exceptionally pleased with it.

(Left) Detail of gutter spine. Photo: Scot Carr

(Right) The bathroom mosaic was designed and assembled by community members. Photo: Alix Henry

MATERIALS TESTING FACILITY
Vancouver, British Columbia
Busby + Associates Architects

General Description
Built on the site of a former asphalt plant, the Materials Testing Facility gives new life to existing materials. Budget constraints and environmental conviction inspired the design team to propose reusing materials from nearby warehouses that were slated for demolition. Rather than burdening a landfill with excess waste and drawing upon the earth's resources for new construction, materials from the existing buildings were salvaged and reconfigured. This strategy made sense environmentally and economically. It also made a powerful statement about the city's priorities and underpinned the building's purpose as a facility for testing materials.

A modified process emerged to confront the difficulties of material-guided design. The design team designated zones throughout the project, and changes were made within each zone according to material availability. Materials dictated the shape, configuration, and composition of the testing facility, which eventually took the form of a two-story rectangular building with testing laboratories downstairs and offices and meeting space upstairs. The team aimed for a 90 percent recycled-content building and achieved a remarkable 80 percent.

(Opposite) Recycled truss expressed on the exterior of the Materials Testing Facility demonstrates the architects' approach to material conservation. Photo: Martin Tessler

Detail of truss base with pin connection. Photo: Martin Tessler

Site

The Materials Testing Facility is located close to the salvaged warehouses. The orientation of the building imparts unobstructed second-floor views toward the Fraser River. This orientation facilitates supervision of the barges that unload gravel at the site.

Earth Strategies

One of the project's early design goals was to use a high percentage of salvaged materials, and this decision shaped the design process. Meeting the objective demanded a flexible and creative team of designers and contractors, because in some cases the architects weren't sure what materials would be available for salvaging. Consequently, the building or portions of it underwent redesign at several points.

The salvageable warehouses at the site had initially been inventoried so as to establish the availability of potentially recyclable materials. From the inventory, the designers developed a recycling specification that addressed the quantity, quality, and storage requirements of materials. The specification included acceptable criteria for each product and warranty, and the

wording ensured a level of design control while allowing greater freedom for the construction manager when procuring the materials. Once the inventory was established, design of the building's form followed. The old large roof trusses were reused to roof the new building. Old gluelams became new roof purlins and a heavy timber floor. Old tongue and groove was converted into roof decking, shear walls, framing studs, and a wood curtain wall. Materials that were not available from the salvaged warehouses were sourced from recycling depots and other buildings scheduled for demolition. Nearly all of the building's components were collected from these sources, including doors, conduits, recycled glass, insulation, metal and wood siding, and lighting and plumbing fixtures.

In addition to reuse, the designers conscientiously applied a strategy of reduction. Exposed structural and mechanical systems eliminated the need for materials with which they are typically concealed. The visible systems also inform the occupants of how the building systems work.

Native plants in nearby drainage swales were protected and maintained, reducing erosion.

Fire Strategies

Ample glazing floods interior spaces with natural light. The roof overhang and roll-down shades help block undesirable direct sun through high windows and prevent it from hitting work spaces. Low windows maintain a connection to the exterior and views of the Fraser River. Clerestory windows in the lab spaces supply a significant amount of natural light.

Air Strategies

The form of the building takes advantage of the local climate and is designed for natural ventilation. Cross ventilation through operable windows eliminates the need for air conditioning. The windows offer occupants control of the immediate environment and permit fresh air to flow through the building. Solar control overhangs reduce demand for cooling. The laboratory areas are isolated and ventilated separately from other occupied spaces in order to maintain air quality. The exhaust fans for the lab components were also salvaged from mills in the area that were being either decommissioned or upgraded. The old drive belts were adjusted for the new task of providing appropriate airflow for the Materials Testing Facility.

Water Strategies

Water from the roof drains first to an oil-and-water separator and then into settlement ponds. After these steps, it is diverted to a 350-foot grassy swale, where it infiltrates slowly rather than increasing the load on the city's stormwater system. Landscaping with native plants minimizes irrigation.

Postscript

From material use to roof runoff, the building presents a positive statement about recycling and reuse applied comprehensively to the architecture. The reuse of materials from an existing structure is one of the most successful aspects of the facility design. Indeed, this building is itself a laboratory, testing the concept of recycling and reusing materials, one of the popular tenets of sustainable architecture. There must have been trade-offs involved with the 80 percent of reused materials that went into the structure. Was the

(Opposite, top) Trusses recall the structure of the adjacent railroad bridge. Photo: Martin Tessler

(Opposite, bottom) Recycled beams are exposed in the building's interior. Photo: Martin Tessler

Clerestory windows provide light and leave walls for casework. Photo: Martin Tessler

The building's exterior clearly differentiates between new and recycled materials. Photo: Martin Tessler

building more difficult, more expensive, or more time-consuming to construct because of this decision? How will the materials perform over the life of the building? Were they easy to install, and are they durable? The decision to reuse materials clearly affected the available material palette, influencing the building's aesthetic. The materials shaped the form and the result was a no-nonsense rectilinear building. But they also seem to have produced a fine level of detailing, with small-scale cladding and structural members. The texture and composition are uncomplicated and refined.

The form of the building also appears to have beneficial implications for natural ventilation and lighting within the building. Do the form and orientation of the building reduce its dependence on nonrenewable energy for operation? Are lights necessary during daylight hours? How has the architecture affected the occupants?

PETITE MAISON DE WEEKEND REVISITED
Patkau Architects

General Description
Throughout the history of architecture, the minimal dwelling has been a vehicle for investigating the basic values of culture and its relationship to technology and the environment. The Petite Maison de Weekend (an allusion to Le Corbusier's weekend retreat in Roquebrune-Cap-Martin, France) is a prototype for a minimal dwelling for our time.

Site
The Petite Maison de Weekend is a portable dwelling unit that can be located on any outdoor site. It is made of a variety of materials and premanufactured components and is designed to be virtually self-sufficient. It provides the basics of habitation: shelter, sleeping loft, kitchen, shower, and composting toilet. The Petite Maison de Weekend generates its own electricity, collects and distributes rainwater, and composts human waste using only the natural dynamics of its site. Basic shelter is provided by a glass and steel roof that measures fourteen by twenty feet.

Earth Strategies
This unit is constructed of materials that are principally renewable or recyclable. The primary material for the structure and shell is hemlock (solid stock and ply). Steel is used at points of concentrated forces, and the roof includes glass. Premanufactured components include photovoltaic panels, batteries, lights, composting toilet, refrigerator, sink, and burner.

Fire Strategies
A photovoltaic array laminated within the central glass units of the roof converts solar radiation into electricity, which is then stored in four deep-cycle batteries. These batteries provide twelve-volt direct current to lights, a high-efficiency refrigerator, and a small fan within the toilet composter. The sleeping loft, which provides accommodation and personal storage for two, is located above the kitchen and composter and is accessible via a fixed aluminum ladder. The kitchen contains a propane-fired burner, a refrigerator, and a sink.

Water Strategies
A fabric reservoir located along the roof's lower edge collects rainwater. The kitchen sink uses water collected from the roof. The shower, which also uses water collected from the roof, is situated directly below the reservoir. The toilet is located above the composter, to the side of the sleeping loft, and is accessible via a split riser stair.

Postscript
This minimal dwelling was designed as a prototype and has received much attention for its innovative design. To date, it has yet to be replicated. The designers learned much from the built project that could be applied to the next iteration. The prototype revealed the need for a design in which components are more independent and independently variable. For instance, the glass-photovoltaic roof could be independently supported with variable

(Opposite) The compact structure of the Petite Maison de Weekend is designed to be completely off the utility grid. Photo: Patkau Architects

Building cross sections (top and middle) and elevation (bottom). Drawing: Patkau Architects

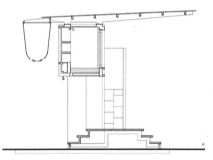

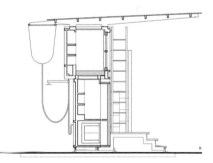

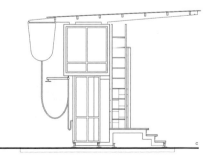

Panels made from hemlock provide the enclosure. Photo: Patkau Architects

components stacked or situated side by side underneath (basically the lesson provided by modular stereo systems). These modifications would allow for a minimal, self-sufficient dwelling with flexibility and simplicity at its core.

The systems, water catchment and solar collection, form the structure's expression. Photo: Patkau Architects

CHAPTER 6

LIGHT AND VENTILATION: CLIMATE-RESPONSIVE ENCLOSURE

ISLANDWOOD
Bainbridge Island, WA
Mithun Architects + Designers + Planners

PIER 56
Seattle, WA
Mithun Architects + Designers + Planners

TELUS/WILLIAM FARRELL BUILDING REVITALIZATION
Vancouver, BC
Busby + Associates Architects

When the history of science is not over-modernized, and Copernicus, for instance, is taken as he was, with all his dreams and ideas, it becomes evident that the stars gravitate about light, and the sun is, primarily, the great Light of the World.

—Gaston Bachelard, *The Poetics of Space*

A fresh breeze, a birdsong, the smell of flowers—as well as the psychological benefits that operable windows provide—are significant. Studies show that people are happier across a much greater temperature range if they have the option of cranking their window open or shut.

—Dianna Lopez Barnett, *A Primer on Sustainable Building*

(Opposite) Suspension system for new glazed wall on the Telus/William Farrell Building provides foreground detail for users. Photo: Martin Tessler

ISLANDWOOD
Bainbridge Island, Washington
Mithun Architects + Designers + Planners

General Description
IslandWood's mission is to teach environmental stewardship to young people by linking ecology, technology, and the arts. It is a place where 4,000 children each year learn about their natural environment. At Island-Wood, the site and the buildings are critical components of the educational curriculum, which aims to teach children about using natural resources more efficiently and the impact we have on the environment.

Project History
Washington State mandates outdoor education for elementary school children, but in 1997, Debbi Brainerd learned that only half of the students receive overnight exposure to a nature-based curriculum. In 1998, after finding a particularly compelling property on the southern end of Bainbridge Island, Debbi and Paul Brainerd collaborated with Mithun and the Berger Partnership, landscape architects, to design a campus for outdoor education. They selected the Bainbridge Island site largely because of its ecological diversity and history of human intervention. Both factors became important components of the curriculum.

Site and Climate
Located at the south end of Bainbridge Island, IslandWood displays both an unusual ecological diversity and a visible legacy of human impact. The site, formerly part of the world's largest lumber mill, now features a pond, a stream, forest, wetlands, and a nearly complete watershed. All of the land comprised by IslandWood was logged at least once, and second-, third-, and fourth-growth forest predominates. The array of landscapes and evidence of human impact provide ample educational opportunities and a range of experiences across the campus.

(Opposite) Children arrive at the IslandWood dining hall. Photo: Roger Williams

Detail of photovoltaic panels and cross bracing at the learning studios. Photo: Roger Williams

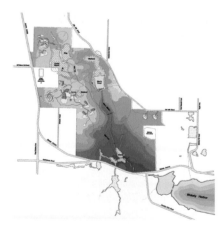

The site offers a fascinating variety of water-land relationships for study. The effects of human presence within the watershed generated a variety of strategies to deal with runoff and reveal the interactions between natural and technical processes. A ravine runs through the middle of the property, forming a drainage corridor to Puget Sound, and provides a unique outdoor classroom. The siting of the buildings preserves the ravine for children's field explorations.

As is typical in the Pacific Northwest, prevailing weather patterns originate in the south, southwest, and west for most of the year, but winds often blow from the north in the summer. The maritime location influences wind, rain, and solar availability. Given existing forest cover and typical weather patterns, maximizing solar access and daylight harvesting became an important goal for the design team; the resulting strategy called for clustering elongated east-west buildings to the north of clearings or solar meadows.

The program consists of twenty-three buildings and sixteen site structures linked by a network of educational trails across a 255-acre campus. Facilities include a welcome center, dining hall, learning studios, Living Machine®, visitors lodges, art studio, staff housing, and maintenance building.

Mithun designed IslandWood to resonate especially from a child's perspective. Early drawings depict the intended experiential sequence of welcome, mystery, discovery, and connection. As visitors move from one activity to another, they connect with the place and its rhythms of landscape and architecture, forest and meadow, exposure and enclosure, natural and human. Building forms incorporate patterns found in nature, and countless details simultaneously engage the imagination and educate.

Earth Strategies

The project team used GIS planning and aerial photography to find the parts of the site that were least disturbed by logging. Mapping of wetlands, soils, and topography indicated sensitive areas, which were set aside for children's field explorations. Areas designated for buildings and solar meadows were carefully marked and cleared. Felled trees became cladding, trim, furniture, and railings. The project team extensively incorporated reused, recycled, or sustainably harvested materials wherever it was feasible.

Elongated in the east-west direction, the buildings at IslandWood maximize the potential for integrating daylighting, passive solar, active solar, and natural ventilation.

Fire Strategies

Many of the buildings employ passive solar strategies for space heating; the learning studio is one example. During the cool seasons, when heating is desirable, the low-angle winter sun enters the circulation corridor through extensive glazing and warms the space, creating a buffer zone for the interior studios. The interior studios can then draw heat from the corridor through a series of operable relites. During the warm seasons, the roof overhang largely shades the corridor, and relites are closed to prevent heat transfer into classrooms.

Photovoltaic roof panels supply 50 percent of the electricity for the learning studios, while solar panels produce 50 percent of the hot water needed for the dining hall and the lodges. The two strategies represent the different energy needs of the buildings. The classroom building requires much less hot water than do the dining hall and lodges, so it makes sense to convert

(Opposite, right) Aerial photo of IslandWood. Photo: Joe Solis

(Opposite, top, left) Site composite map. Maps by Mithun

(Opposite, middle, left) Wetlands map

(Opposite, bottom, left) Site composite map

Learning studio section depicts daylight, active and passive solar, natural ventilation, and rainwater harvesting. Drawing: Mithun

(Bottom) Plan of learning studios, elongated in the east-west direction for optimal solar conditions. Drawing: Mithun

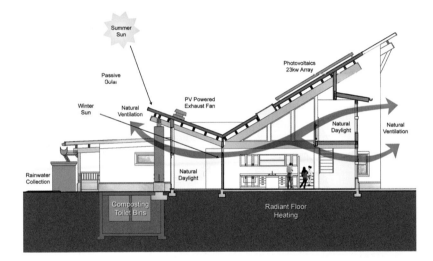

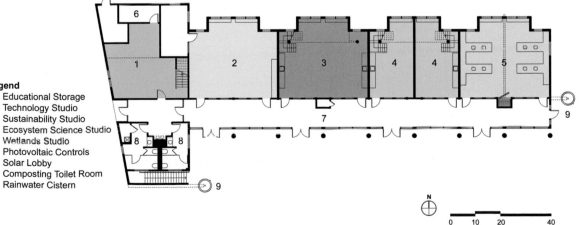

Legend
1. Educational Storage
2. Technology Studio
3. Sustainability Studio
4. Ecosystem Science Studio
5. Wetlands Studio
6. Photovoltaic Controls
7. Solar Lobby
8. Composting Toilet Room
9. Rainwater Cistern

the sun's heat energy into electricity there. Storing the sun's heat as hot water is more efficient than converting it to electricity in buildings that consume greater quantities of hot water.

Daylight enters the buildings largely from the north and south, which are optimum orientations. Skylights bring daylight into the middle of interior spaces and help balance the overall light levels laterally. Daylight reduces the need for electric lights, contributing significantly to energy conservation.

Air Strategies

Wind direction studies informed building orientation, which was designed to capitalize on the opportunity for natural ventilation. With the exception of spot ventilation for the bathrooms, kitchen, and auditorium, the buildings are completely naturally ventilated. Photovoltaic-powered exhaust fans assist the natural ventilation scheme. Other air quality measures include minimizing interior finishes (and their accompanying emissions) and installing carbon dioxide monitors.

Water Strategies

IslandWood features water as an important educational tool; man's treatment of water runs alongside natural streams, wetlands, and a lake, demonstrating our place within and effect on natural patterns. Careful planning and engineering of on-site water treatment strategies make it unnecessary to connect to the municipal sewage system. A Living Machine® at the educational core treats both gray and black water for reuse using biological processes, while a subsurface-flow constructed wetland treats wastewater at the lodges and the graduate student housing. Other water conservation strategies include rainwater harvesting, composting toilets, low-flow water fixtures, native plants (which thrive on natural patterns of precipitation), and study of wetland habitat.

Postscript

The diversity and complexity of the sustainable strategies at IslandWood are a fitting architectural counterpoint to the site's ecological diversity. Just as the site is conceptualized as a teacher, so, too, are the buildings, offering endless opportunities for learning and discovery. The sheer variety of sustainable strategies that are skillfully displayed and employed at Island-Wood, while arguably one of the most meaningful measures of success

(Top, left) Schematic diagram of possible solar strategies. Drawing: Keen Engineering

(Bottom, left) Learning studio with north operable windows. Photo: Doug Scott

(Bottom, right) Wastewater treatment diagram. Drawing: Mithun

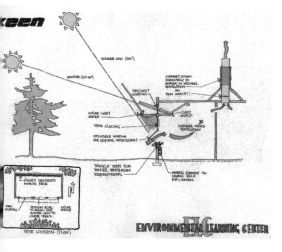

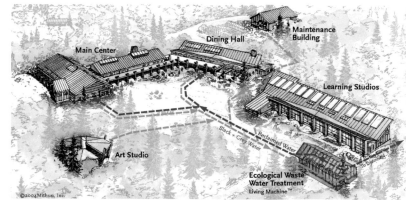

for this type of project, is also a potential drawback. The buildings and systems require constant adjustments for optimal performance and comfort. A rotating staff and a continually changing population of visitors must have periodic training in order to maximize operating efficiencies.

Beyond an operational understanding, ongoing evaluation is needed in order to gauge how well the sustainable strategies are actually performing. Quantitatively, how much energy is being saved? Which strategies provide the greatest savings? How much water is used and treated? Qualitatively, are occupants comfortable? If not, is the discomfort due to a lack of operational understanding, the failure of a designed system, or an acceptable fluctuation? Ongoing studies, using meters set up for data collection, will not only inform the staff and visitors at IslandWood but also contribute to the knowledge base on the effectiveness of specific sustainable strategies in the Pacific Northwest.

The common dilemma of measured performance versus qualitative experience is one example of many ongoing discussions within the field of sustainable design. Monitoring revealed that the photovoltaic installation on the roof of the learning studios did not achieve full power output. Designed for direct southern exposure in the solar meadow, the installation was compromised by a patch of morning shade on the east end of the building created by a specimen big-leaf maple. Although the tree enhances the beauty and majesty of the users' experience, it reduces the efficiency of the energy collection system. The debate over whether or not to remove the tree continues. Either choice entails a trade-off.

The potential positive impact of IslandWood is difficult to calculate but could be significant. In addition to all the lives inspired by the powerful educational experience, IslandWood holds a wealth of information that could be used to improve the efficacy of sustainable design in our region.

(Left) Living Machine® treats wastewater on-site. Photo: Doug J. Scott/ dougscott.com

(Right) Detail of gutter at cistern. Photo: Susan Olmsted

PIER 56
Seattle, Washington
Mithun Architects + Designers + Planners

General Description

Mithun Architects + Designers + Planners was growing and in need of new office space. At the same time, the historic Pier 56 on Seattle's waterfront stood vacant, in need of renovation and reoccupation. Mithun's adaptive reuse of Pier 56 preserved an important historic structure and integrated its vision for a sustainable working environment. For Mithun, a sustainable working environment meant reducing water and energy consumption, improving air quality, increasing connections to the outside, and encouraging social interaction.

Mithun organized its second-floor open office environment along a conceptual Main Street. As employees or visitors walk along this Main Street, they may view recent Mithun projects on display, stop by a project pin-up, visit the model shop, meet a colleague, or have lunch. The various office departments are arranged to encourage movement and interaction, a strategy Mithun feels improves employee relations and the overall office environment. Open communication and collaboration among employees are of vital importance for a firm that focuses on sustainable design. The office itself is considered a laboratory for testing new ideas, technologies, and

(Opposite) Pier 56 and Seattle from Elliott Bay. Photo: Roger Williams

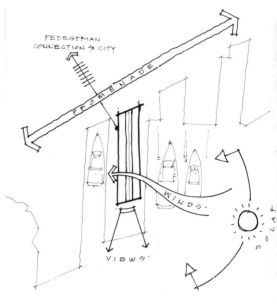

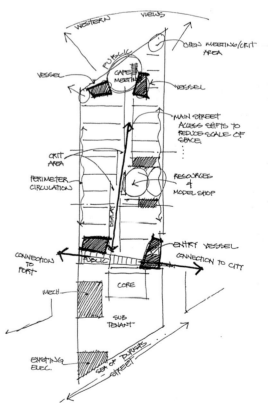

(Preceding page, left) Operable windows, both high and low, supply the office interior with daylight, views, and fresh air. Photo: Robert Pisano

(Preceding page, top, right) Schematic diagram of site characteristics. Drawing: Mithun

(Preceding page, bottom, right) Schematic diagram of Main Street concept. Drawing: Mithun

Historical photo of Pier 56. Photo: Paul Dorpat

materials that help improve sustainable performance and inspire employees at their work.

Earth Strategies
Mithun perceives its office as a testing ground for renewable, reused, and recycled materials. As such, it is particularly fitting that the office is housed in a renovated historic structure, all of which was salvaged and left unfinished. Other materials include exposed steel reinforcements, formaldehyde-free prefinished plywood, OSB flooring, salvaged sample tiles, and low-VOC finishes and glues.

Fire Strategies
The light of the sky enters through clerestory and side windows, supplying daylight and connecting employees to the natural cycles of the day and the season. In summer, the direct sun heats the high clerestory, creating a temperature differential between the high clerestory and the occupied space. The difference in temperature accelerates air movement and aids cooling.

Air Strategies
The ventilation strategy uses operable windows, both side and clerestory (with cranks). Cool air from off the water's surface enters side windows, moves across the space, and rises up and out at the clerestory, displacing heat. Powered fans assist the movement of air through the space. Each employee is taught how to operate the system. Along with fresh air, the open windows provide visual and auditory connections to the sights and sounds of the waterfront.

Other air quality measures include using low-VOC finishes and glues, formaldehyde-free prefinished plywood, and other recycled and renewable materials throughout the building.

Environmentally friendly materials lead the way along the office's Main Street. The final destination offers a panoramic view of the water. Photo: Robert Pisano

(Bottom) Section of building depicts natural ventilation and key sustainable strategies. Drawing: Mithun

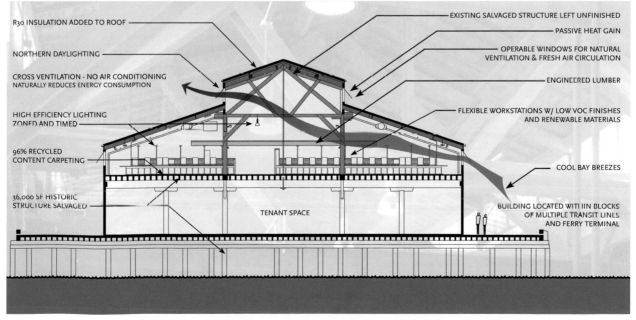

R30 INSULATION ADDED TO ROOF

NORTHERN DAYLIGHTING

CROSS VENTILATION - NO AIR CONDITIONING
NATURALLY REDUCES ENERGY CONSUMPTION

HIGH EFFICIENCY LIGHTING
ZONED AND TIMED

96% RECYCLED
CONTENT CARPETING

36,000 SF HISTORIC
STRUCTURE SALVAGED

EXISTING SALVAGED STRUCTURE LEFT UNFINISHED

PASSIVE HEAT GAIN

OPERABLE WINDOWS FOR NATURAL
VENTILATION & FRESH AIR CIRCULATION

ENGINEERED LUMBER

FLEXIBLE WORKSTATIONS W/ LOW VOC FINISHES
AND RENEWABLE MATERIALS

COOL BAY BREEZES

BUILDING LOCATED WITHIN BLOCKS
OF MULTIPLE TRANSIT LINES
AND FERRY TERMINAL

TENANT SPACE

Cool marine air helps maintain interior comfort. Photo: Roger Williams

(Bottom) Manually operated gears open the sash for ventilation. Photo: Mithun

Of course, the pier is well connected to the water. The most impressive views of Puget Sound, waves, mountains, and boats have been preserved as shared space. The lunchroom serves as the final destination in the Main Street environment, a place to meet, take a break, or enjoy the view and reconnect with the world outside. The sights, sounds, and smells of the water encourage consciousness of its value as a resource and underscore the importance of conservation. Strategies employed to help conserve water include low-flush toilets and fixtures.

Postscript

The concept of an office as a laboratory corresponds well with Mithun's commitment to sustainability. Ongoing testing of new materials, products, and strategies allows Mithun to experience firsthand the performance and effectiveness of alternatives. If a product fails, the company learns why and can either make adjustments or turn to a different product.

For example, Mithun tried waterless urinals in the restrooms for a period of time, but although the urinals had been used successfully with other projects, the fixtures did not work at Pier 56. Through the product failure, Mithun discovered a key detail for proper application: the urinals should not be placed at the end of the plumbing line. Proper functioning requires the flushing of other appliances or fixtures upstream. The waterless urinals were replaced with other experimental, water-conserving fixtures.

The natural ventilation scheme is another example of ongoing testing. Over time, employees noticed that certain locations within the office received more airflow than others. They also determined the patterns of cool air and heat rejection throughout the day. With these observations, they were able to develop optimum strategies for maximizing the effectiveness of the natural ventilation scheme. Precooling the office in the morning hours helped offset the heat of the late afternoon. Although the office temperature is allowed to fluctuate within a greater range than most, it never exceeds a tolerable level, even during the peak of summer. The natural cooling of the marine air and an office culture that supports a seasonal dress code (i.e., shorts) contribute to the comfort of employees.

Mithun employees inhabit a space that inspires and informs their work. Their experience with the types of strategies and products they specify for others enables them to make educated decisions. Ongoing evaluation reinforces the idea that the path toward sustainability, like all good design, requires a continual influx of current information and the willingness to reassess the path taken.

TELUS/WILLIAM FARRELL BUILDING REVITALIZATION
Vancouver, British Columbia
Busby + Associates Architects

General Description

In 1998, Telus, a communications company, wanted to establish a strong presence in downtown Vancouver while accommodating the changing needs of a growing business. The project catalyst was the early decision to revitalize the existing William Farrell Building; the course was strongly directed toward sustainability. The resulting solution integrates conceptual, technical, aesthetic, and environmental goals for the project. A new glazed skin is suspended from the previously existing concrete shell, forming a sleek double-skin facade and presenting a futuristic new image to the public. The double skin greatly increases the technical performance of the building envelope and has the added advantage of permitting direct occupant control. The increased technical performance reduces operational energy, multiplying the environmental benefits already achieved by recycling an existing structure and minimizing new construction.

Site and Climate

The Telus building is located in downtown Vancouver, on a highly visible lot with good sun exposure. The sun exposure became a critical consideration for design team members as they aimed to generate an energy- and resource-efficient solution. Shifting urban wind patterns dictated flexibility for the purpose of maintaining natural ventilation. The resulting double-skin solution is adaptable to site, solar, and other climate conditions and responsive to occupant needs.

On the neighborhood scale, the Telus building optimizes resource use by utilizing waste heat from the adjacent refrigeration plant; 52 percent of the plant's waste heat supplies 100 percent of the building's heating needs. One structure's waste becomes another structure's resource. The project reduced impact to the immediate property by recycling an existing building, which additionally reduced impact to the surrounding region by decreasing embodied energy consumption. On the neighborhood scale, cooperation between adjacent buildings provides mutual benefits to each building as well as to the city.

Earth Strategies

Recycling the existing concrete structure saved 16,000 tons of solid waste landfill and avoided 15,600 tons of greenhouse gas emissions. The project team also found ways to recycle many of the existing interior components, including air handling units and piping; the elevator shaft, cabs, and machinery; windows, doors, frames, hardware, stairs, guardrails, light fittings, marble water-closet partitions, and office furniture; and granite cladding on two ground stories. The William Farrell Building provided 115,000 square feet of space above grade. Regulations dictated that a new building on the site could provide only 70,000 square feet of space, generating a loss of 45,000 square feet of urban space. By electing not to construct a new building, the design team maintained the density of the site, maximized the efficiency of the building footprint, and prevented sprawl onto another location.

(Page 116) Overview of the Telus/ William Farrell Building, downtown Vancouver. Photo: Martin Tessler

(Preceding page, top) Corner detail of double-glazed skin. Photo: Martin Tessler

(Preceding page, bottom) Installation of new glazed skin over the existing building. Photo: Martin Tessler

(Right) Air cavity modulates the building's temperature. Photo: Martin Tessler

Fire Strategies

The double-glazed skin uses the sun to optimize thermal performance. During cool seasons, the cavity traps the sun's heat as it radiates through the glass. Supply air enters through the cavity and is warmed by the trapped heat, reducing the energy needed for heating. Occupants draw directly upon the heated cavity by opening interior windows. During the warm seasons, the cavity, which has dampers at the top and bottom, generates a stack effect, whereby cool air enters low and then rises as it heats up. This increases air movement through the space. Occupants have the option of opening windows on the exterior and interior in order to bring in additional

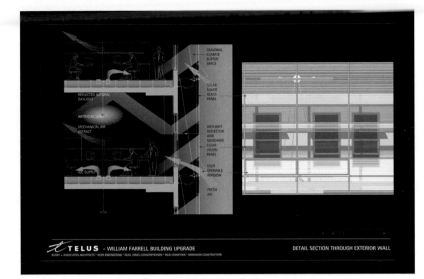

fresh air and increase flushing. Photovoltaic-assisted fans integrated with the glazed skin supply active solar energy to run fans that assist in ventilation. Light shelves maximize the perimeter of light available to interior spaces. Strategically placed ceramic frit glass blocks the undesirable direct summer sun but allows low-angle winter sun penetration through to the interior. The associated winter solar gain supplements required heating. The thermal mass of the existing concrete shell absorbs heat throughout the day and slowly reradiates it at a later time. This thermal lag shifts peak cooling, reducing the overall load and benefiting the city grid.

Air Strategies

A tensile steel structural system supports the double glazing that wraps the concrete shell. The resulting cavity, a thirty-six-inch atrium, circulates fresh air for ventilation. Occupants of the building maintain direct control over the operable windows on the old shell and the new skin, which enables them to modify their immediate environment and achieve individual comfort.

The raised floor plenum system for circulating fresh air to the work spaces furthers the individual occupant's ability to control the environment. The system allows maximum flexibility for a frequently changing office configuration, and employees may adjust airflow to suit their needs. The system also saves energy by supplying air directly to occupied spaces at a lower velocity and a more moderate temperature than is provided by traditional forced air systems.

Postscript

By taking an existing structure and modifying it for contemporary needs, the Telus building embodies creative and innovative solutions to sustainable design. What are the trade-offs? The form was set, and the architects were required to fit the programming within the existing structure. Light shelves and large areas of glazing were optimized so as to bring in daylight. Inventive mechanical systems take advantage of the large embodied energy of the existing massive structure. The decision to reuse undoubtedly affected

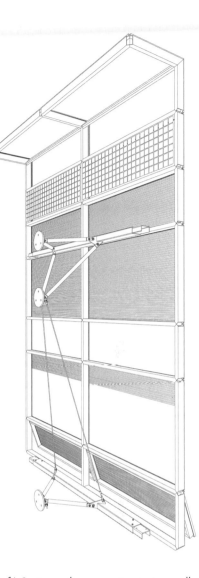

(Left) Systems diagram at exterior wall. Drawing: Busby + Associates

(Right) Detail of tensile steel structural support for the glazed skin. Drawing: Busby + Associates

*Heating and cooling diagram. Draw-
ing: Keen Engineering*

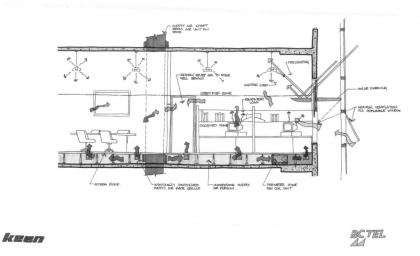

the aesthetics of the renovation. A formerly blocky and bulky structure is
now shiny and sleek with large expanses of glass, yet the building seems to
hold onto its heavy stance. Each facade remains as a large plane, without
considerable articulation or dimension.

The Telus building is a unique case study in the Pacific Northwest
because of the double-skin facade that incorporates operable windows to
provide natural ventilation. The design assigns responsibility to the occupants for control of their immediate environment through operation of the
windows and vents in the plenum. Does such a design empower or compli-
cate the person's connection to the architecture? In reality, it educates users
about climate control in buildings and enhances working conditions with
improved individual comfort.

The architecture sets out to reduce energy use by means of these systems
in combination with the thermal mass of the structure. Tracking this energy
consumption and comparing it with the building's energy demand prior to
the renovation could impart some clues about the value of this solution. The
Telus/William Farrell Building is an excellent model for double-skin sustainable design strategies for large multistory structures.

Double-skin air cavity. Photo: Martin Tessler

CHAPTER 7

TECHNOLOGY AND MATERIALS: THE INTEGRATED FUTURE

SEATTLE JUSTICE CENTER AND SEATTLE CIVIC CENTER PLAN
Seattle, WA
NBBJ Architects

BAINBRIDGE ISLAND CITY HALL
Bainbridge, WA
The Miller/Hull Partnership

PEARL DISTRICT
Portland, OR
Jean Vollum Natural Capital Center, Holst Architecture
The Brewery Blocks, GDB Architects and Gerding/Edlen Development
Wieden + Kennedy Building, Allied Works Architecture

The essence of what has been done to temper the environment has been—at every single stage—the displacement of habit by experiment, and of accepted custom by informed innovation. The greatest of all environmental powers is thought, and the usefulness of thought, the very reason for applying radical intelligence to our problems, is precisely that it dissolves what architecture has been made to date: Customary forms.

—Reyner Banham, *The Architecture of the Well-Tempered Environment*

(Opposite) Atrium space in the Wieden + Kennedy Building. Photo: Sally Schoolmaster

SEATTLE JUSTICE CENTER AND SEATTLE CIVIC CENTER PLAN
Seattle, Washington
NBBJ Architects

General Description

The Seattle Justice Center, the first structure in a three-block new civic core, replaced the outmoded and seismically deficient Public Safety Building, which was torn down only fifty years after it was built. The new Civic Center Plan called for a longer lifespan, 100 years, situating sustainability at the forefront of new development. If it was to last at least 100 years, the Seattle Justice Center needed to satisfy a challenging array of criteria, both for today and for tomorrow. NBBJ selected the following as predominant: to achieve a minimum LEED silver rating, to illustrate a clear distinction between the police headquarters and the city courthouse, to maintain flexibility for future growth, to make an aesthetic contribution to the city, and to reveal the accessibility of the judicial process. These goals translated into a bipartite strategy. A more solid, stone police block to the north was juxtaposed with a transparent judicial block to the south. At the joint between the two blocks ran a waterfall, the origin of a three-block conceptual link to ideas of urban ecology within the overall Civic Center Plan. The largely west-facing edge of the site presented a significant challenge because of its difficult solar orientation; the idea for the double-glazed skin along the west facade emerged as a strategy for reconciling ideas of transparency with the mandate of sustainability.

Site and Climate

The Seattle Justice Center is the first installation of a three-part plan for the civic center, as designed by landscape architects Gustafson Guthrie Nichols, Ltd. The plan links the Seattle Justice Center, the city hall, and the public safety and administrative offices along the path of a metaphorical urban waterway. The waterway is intended to express urban topography as well as regional hydrology, moving from east to west, from high to low, from the "mountains" to the "sound." Public open spaces associated with each phase are terraced with the flow of the water and benefit from the southern and western orientations that maximize solar access and views. Considered within the context of this larger urban plan, the available views, and the physical constraints of its site (an existing parking garage dominated the eastern portion), it was necessary that the Seattle Justice Center face west. The west facade thus became the public expression of the transparency and accessibility of the judicial process, a difficult orientation for controlling the heat and glare of the sun.

The highly visible urban location presented the opportunity to reach a wide variety of people with the message of sustainability. The idea that a building can reveal site conditions through architectural response is inherent to sustainability. The double-glazed skin and the stormwater runoff strategy became two key ways to emphasize local conditions and urban ecology. The aforementioned challenging western orientation evoked the double-skin response, while annual rainfall and the urban heat-island effect influenced water strategies and roof composition.

(Opposite) Seattle Justice Center from James Street. Photo: Christian Richters

Architect's sketch of double-skin concept. Drawing: NBBJ

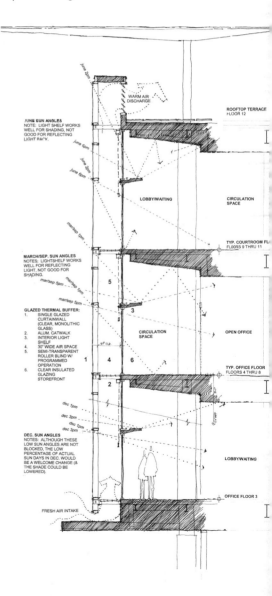

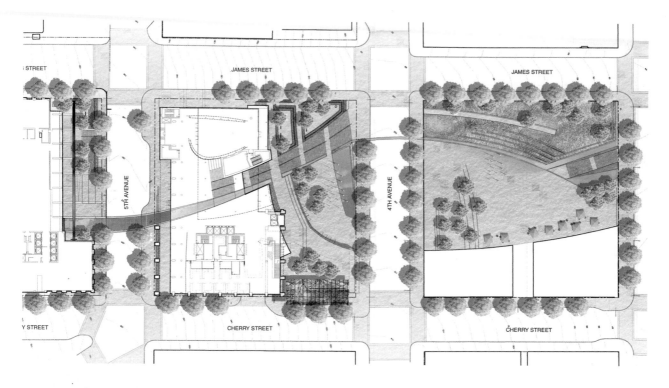

Civic Center Plan. Drawing: GGN Landscape Architects

(Bottom) West facade shows layering of double skin. Photo: Tim Griffith

Fire Strategies

For a project that proactively stated its aspirations with regard to sustainability, the aforementioned transparent west facade presented a significant challenge. The low, rapidly changing solar angles contributed by the western path of the sun make glare and heat transfer crucial issues for west-facing glass. In response, NBBJ, in cooperation with engineers Ove Arup and Partners, designed a double-skin glazed thermal buffer, turning the difficult orientation into an architectural asset. Though comparable double-skin systems are prevalent in Europe, there are to date relatively few installations in the United States. Recognizing the potential for construction error, and with the intent of minimizing the cost, the entire system is made of standard materials and utilized common building techniques. The system, from outside to inside, is composed of a curtain wall system with clear, monolithic glazing; a thirty-inch air cavity with aluminum catwalks at each floor level; programmed semitransparent roll-down shades; and insulated, clear storefront glazing with an internal light shelf.

The vented double-skin facade maximizes transparency, views, and daylight while minimizing heat transfer and glare. Calculations and data analysis revealed that the critical issue for the Seattle Justice Center was solar heat gain. The thirty-inch cavity between layers of glazing traps heat, reducing the transfer of heat from the exterior to the interior and vice versa. During warm seasons, when cooling is necessary, apertures at the top and bottom of the cavity induce air movement, as hot air rises and cool air enters low. During the cool seasons, when heating is necessary, the air cavity can be sealed at the top, and the cavity becomes an insulating buffer between the warm interior and the cool exterior. The ability to control the apertures, and thus the movement or capture of heat, allows the cavity to mediate between interior and exterior temperatures.

Another advantage of the glazed double skin is that it incorporates shading devices. In a typical glazed or curtain wall assembly, roll-down shades are positioned on the interior surface of the glazing. While this positioning reduces glare from the direct sun, it also reduces the assembly's effectiveness at shielding the glass from solar gain. In a double-skin assembly, the shades can be positioned on the exterior surface of the inner layer of glass, thus shielding against the sun's glare and heat more effectively. In addition to roll-down shades, the buffer wall integrates catwalks and light shelves to help shade from direct sun and to bounce daylight deeper into the space.

Air Strategies

As described above, the buffer wall utilizes stack ventilation, whereby temperature stratification increases airflow and helps to flush the cavity during times when cooling is desirable. Cool air enters low, rises with the increase in temperature, and then exits through louvers at the top of the cavity. The displacement caused by the transfer of heat fuels the continual flow of air from low to high. The louvers can be programmed and adjusted to flush or contain the air within the cavity, according to varying conditions.

NBBJ selected materials and finishes that contribute to healthy air quality. No-VOC materials were used throughout, and VAV box filters minimized the accumulation of construction dust in air ducts. Prior to occupation, a two-week air-flush period further helped ensure good air quality.

Water Strategies

The metaphorical path of the water mentioned above became the strategy for addressing stormwater runoff as well as connecting the three phases of the Civic Center Plan. The path begins atop the Seattle Justice Center as a vegetated roof planted with flowing mounds of blue fescue and sedum. Beyond providing the conceptual impetus for the urban river, the plants absorb rainfall and reduce runoff. From the roof, a cascade of glass situated between the stone police block and the transparent judicial block carries the idea of the water to the plaza below, where an actual pool bubbles and gurgles, reinforcing the metaphor. The idea continues across the street to the city hall, becoming a light shaft that runs from east to west across another vegetated roof and then a series of public terraces that culminates in another pool. A similar condition for the Public Safety and Administration Building completes the triptych. GGN Ltd. carefully orchestrated the slopes of hard surfaces to drain toward planting beds or, in the case of the city hall plaza, toward the water pool, further reducing runoff.

The Civic Center Plan also calls for the collection and storage of water. The Seattle Justice Center incorporates a below-grade rainwater harvesting tank that collects runoff and stores it for irrigation purposes, as does the adjacent new City Hall. Although the tanks do not have the capacity to meet all irrigation needs, they do provide a significant supplement.

Postscript

The Civic Center Plan in general and the Seattle Justice Center in particular place issues of urban ecology in a prominent position. The integration of the overall plan within the urban fabric, the links between the three buildings and their adjacent public spaces, and the incorporation of sustainable

Interior circulation along window wall with light shelves. Photo: Christian Richters

(Bottom) Glass cascade at entrance. Photo: Tim Griffith

The building's green roof is visible from adjacent windows. Photo: Christian Richters

(Bottom) Seattle Justice Center plaza. Photo: Christian Richters

strategies all illustrate growing consciousness of the potential of the built environment to contribute to the overall health of its people and to connect with natural systems. Two of the three phases have been constructed to date, and initial qualitative surveys of Seattle Justice Center occupants have revealed a largely positive response. People like working there, and they appreciate the views. Even so, glare has been an ongoing concern, especially for those who work on the first floor. The idea of openness and transparency, while possibly improving public relations, makes for a harsh interior work space in locations where there is little or no protection from the direct rays and bright reflections of the sun. In this case, the idea might have met with greater functional success had it been a bit more flexible in its application. Over time, the trees planted on the west side will grow tall enough to help shade the first floor.

Other problem areas have been reported, mostly related to glare and direct sun on exposed perimeter work spaces. NBBJ and Ove Arup performed exhaustive studies of the double-glazed buffer system, including daylighting and energy modeling. The extensive study expended on this important feature, though crucial to the success of the project, was performed at the expense of some of the other areas throughout the building. Occupants report frustration with the automated roll-down shades, and ad hoc shading devices decorate many of the workstations. This margin of dissatisfaction underscores varying individual preferences and sensitivities and reflects the constraints of a tight budget, strict operational requirements, and admirable goals.

As for the performance of the glazed thermal buffer, quantitative analysis has begun, although conclusions were not available at the time of publication. Regardless of initial results, ongoing analysis is needed to determine the effectiveness of the strategy and its components. It must be emphasized, however, that without the buffer wall, the Seattle Justice Center would be compelled to compromise on transparency and accessibility.

The Seattle Justice Center stands as the first real test of the city's goal to achieve a LEED silver rating on all new civic buildings. Lessons learned from this groundbreaking application will improve the success of future efforts, furthering our awareness of the potential for a sustainable built environment.

Top of double-skin facade, with city beyond. Photo: Christian Richters

BAINBRIDGE ISLAND CITY HALL
Bainbridge Island, Washington
The Miller/Hull Partnership

General Description

The newly incorporated city of Bainbridge Island needed a new city hall that would bring together five dispersed departments under one roof and enable a more efficient operation. The Miller/Hull Partnership, along with environmental design consultants O'Brien & Company, developed a plan that not only provided efficient operations but also stretched the limits of sustainable design. Multiuse space became a key strategy for reducing the size of the building. As designed, workrooms and meeting rooms are shared, and much of the office space is open. This consolidation strategy extends outside the building, where three groups of users with different parking demands share the site. Analysis of the different needs and patterns of use inspired the idea of using a reinforced turf system. During the week, the space serves as public green for the city hall. On the weekend, it becomes the Farmers' Market, and in the evening, it serves as overflow parking for the performing arts center. In addition to efficient programming and space planning, the building integrates a number of other sustainable features, including daylighting, environmentally sensitive materials and finishes, responsible landscaping, and stormwater improvements.

Earth Strategies

Bainbridge Island City Hall occupies the former site of a gas station and gravel parking lot, which required extensive cleanup of hazardous waste

(Opposite) Bainbridge Island City Hall from Madison Street. Photo: Art Grice

Pedestrian bench detail. Photo: Art Grice

(Bottom) Site plan. Drawing: Miller/ Hull

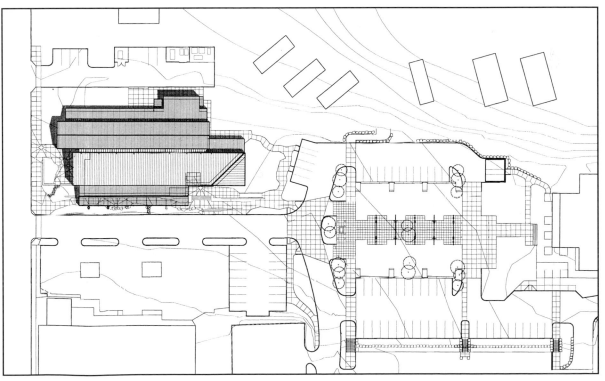

from empty gas tanks and contaminated soil prior to construction. Now people, native plants, and architecture create a safe, lively public realm on this once toxic location.

Material selection played a key role in reinforcing the City's commitment to sustainability. The structure utilized 70,000 board feet of FSC-certified wood for framing, and gluelams provided the desired proportion and spanning capabilities, which saved old-growth forests. Other sustainable and recycled materials include fiberglass insulation with 25 percent recycled-content glass, gypsum wallboard with 18 percent recycled-content gypsum, acoustical tile with 69 percent recycled-content fiber, plastic toilet partitions and locker-room benches with 100 percent recycled content, recyclable carpet that can be converted to new carpet at the end of its useful lifespan, and resource-efficient fiberboard with longer life and lower maintenance requirements. In addition, concrete and asphalt waste was recycled during site development.

Fire Strategies
Skylights and side-lights introduce daylight. The open office plan in conjunction with light-colored interiors maximizes the amount of daylight available to interior spaces. Daylight reduces dependency on electric lighting, and multiple switching (zones) further saves energy. Large overhangs help shade the windows, minimizing heat gain.

Water Strategies

A variety of strategies minimized the overall impact of the city hall on surrounding waterways. The selection of a previously developed site on an in-fill lot in town increased the density of the town center and alleviated the potential impact on outlying areas. Cleanup of the contaminated soil and materials on-site provided a safe path for water infiltration and prevented leaching of harmful chemicals into surrounding soils and waterways. The installation of porous paving further improved groundwater infiltration and reduced site runoff, while native plants minimize irrigation requirements. The City's stormwater management system was also significantly upgraded during site preparation.

(Opposite, top) The Farmers' Market shares the parking lot on weekends. Photo: Art Grice

(Opposite, bottom) Resource cabinet at entry contains maps and photos for public use. Photo: Art Grice

(Left) Interior design maximizes daylight in the public space. Photo: Art Grice

(Right) Schematic section. Drawing: Bob Hull

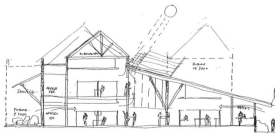

Exterior shared space with steel armatures for market stalls. Photo: Art Grice

(Bottom) Building floor plan. Drawing: Miller/Hull

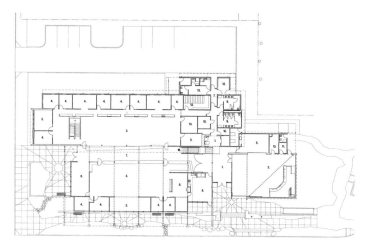

Postscript

Bainbridge Island is a wooded retreat, just a short ferry ride away from Seattle, and island residents appreciate the balance of forest and village that defines its semirural lifestyle. The Bainbridge Island City Hall resonates with both the landscape and the historic, utilitarian forms. Its understated form is a reinterpretation of the island vernacular, and Miller/Hull's use of environmentally friendly materials and strategies reveals sensitivity to its users and setting. This deceptively simple building is a testament to rigorous programmatic and functional analysis, an important example of how architecture can adeptly serve its community.

From the inception of the project, the design team worked to integrate sustainable strategies but always remained conscious of the budget. Understanding the strategies that generate multiple benefits, or achieving the greatest contribution for a given capital input, requires careful planning. Thus, most of the green aspects of the project are elements integral to form or function. For example, windows provide views, daylight, and fresh air, and their positioning reinforces the logic of the structure. Low operable windows on the south admit fresh air, while high operable windows on the

north encourage air circulation throughout the building. A series of interior operable windows between the lower south side and the higher north side (just below the skylights) contributes permeability between spaces with the intent that opening or closing the windows would allow users to alter the dynamics of acoustics and airflow to suit their needs. It must be stressed, however, that no studies have been undertaken to date to evaluate the success of this scenario. Although this strategy reflects the intent to increase occupant comfort and control via simple, cost-effective measures, the natural aspects of the ventilation system could perhaps have been pushed further.

Multiplicity of function, or the ability of one space to serve various users, might be the least visible though most effective sustainable strategy of this project. Rather than build five different spaces to serve five different groups of people, Miller/Hull planned to provide one flexible space that could be shared. The council meeting room is adaptable to many purposes. This sharing of space conserves resources, both natural and economic. In this case, it decreased the building footprint significantly, an aspect that reinforced notions about the island setting.

JEAN VOLLUM NATURAL CAPITAL CENTER (ECOTRUST)
Pearl District, Portland, Oregon
Holst Architecture

Site

North of downtown Portland, within the larger River District and the city's former warehouse and railyard area, lies the district now affectionately known as the Pearl. The Pearl District, with its historic brick buildings and 100 acres of waterfront, has recently undergone extensive redevelopment, changing from an underutilized neighborhood of struggling businesses and transients to a vital and vibrant link to the downtown core. The area is a model of the type of development that is also occurring in other cities throughout the Pacific Northwest. As these cities strive for greater density within the urban core, and as manufacturing is displaced by high-tech, former industrial neighborhoods adjacent to the civic core become prime localities for transformation. This phenomenon can be seen in Vancouver's Granville Island, Tacoma's museum district and University of Washington campus, and more recently in Seattle's South Lake Union neighborhood. These neighborhoods address critical questions of preserving and enhancing regional identity within a changing demographic. Portland's Pearl District, with its emphasis on sustainable redevelopment, illustrates many of the strategies that are being enlisted elsewhere throughout the Pacific Northwest and that work well in defining its unique conditions.

At the metropolitan scale, Portland has enacted a couple of interesting planning strategies that affect development. First, the urban growth boundary intensifies development within the city while minimizing sprawl. This is a complex issue, and although it is not the focus of this case study, it is important to mention as part of a larger political construct. Second, the city adheres to a composition of blocks that measure 200 by 200 feet. This small-block arrangement serves the pedestrian particularly well, with greater surface area for storefronts and improved walkability compared to a larger-block construct.

At the neighborhood scale, Portland's Pearl District has set the stage for a healthy community. Transportation alternatives, mixed-use development, lush landscaping, public open space, and a pedestrian scale invite

(Opposite) Interior lobby with new structure inserted into the existing historic building. Photo: Dan Tyrpak

(Left) Public transit serves the district. Photo: Dan Tyrpak

(Right) External steel seismic bracing. Photo: Dan Tyrpak

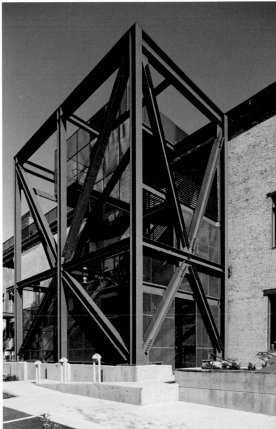

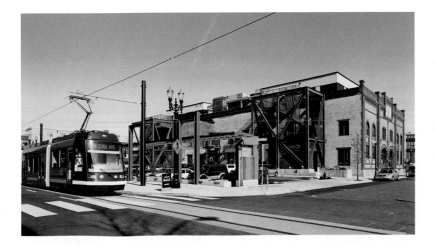

A new mixed-use building by Ankrom Moisan reflects some of its art deco neighbors in the Pearl District. Photo: David Miller

(Bottom) Map of Pearl District

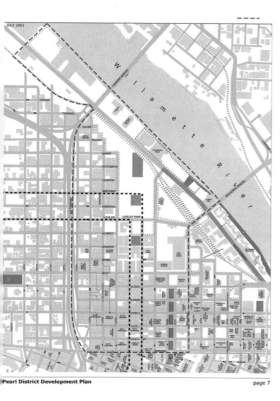

people to use and occupy its streets and structures. Within this construct of short blocks, through-block passageways, and green edges, individual buildings display forward steps in sustainable design. Especially intriguing are historic structures such as the breweries, cold storage facilities, and warehouses that have been adapted to new functions. Adaptive reuse has the twofold benefit of resource efficiency and preservation of regional and historic character.

The Pearl District contains a number of buildings that have contributed significantly to the growing ideology regarding sustainable adaptation of historic structures. Underscoring the inherent variability in this line of work, each existing structure held unique challenges and opportunities that resulted in site- and project-specific design solutions. As with any architectural endeavor, particularly in the field of sustainability, trade-offs were part of the process. Budget, time, resource availability, and advances in building technology all played key roles in determining the resultant architectural manifestation. Equally as applicable now as then, the way we build exemplifies the natural, social, political, and economic construct of a particular region. Ultimately, the adapted Pearl District buildings become physical demarcations of the transformation of a locality and its population over time.

This building and the two also examined below incorporate a host of sustainable strategies that contribute to the health and livability of the Pearl District. All are heavily laden with the innovative use of recycled materials, low-VOC finishes, and various green building practices, underscoring the growing acceptance of sustainability as part of Portland's contribution to a new regional identity within an historical construct. Many of the district's newly renovated buildings have planted green roofs. With the intent of reducing repetition, the discussion of these projects will center on the more unique and expressive of their sustainable strategies.

General Description

The Jean Vollum Natural Capital Center (JVNCC), developed by Ecotrust and designed by Holst Architecture, occupies a former warehouse built in 1887. Beyond the exhaustive list of recycled materials and green construction practices, this project is especially noteworthy in its expression of earth and water. It also offers an instructive example in its struggle with solar access.

Earth Strategies

When Holst Architecture began the process of adapting the warehouse to new use, designers confronted the requirements of modern seismic codes. The 1887 masonry warehouse needed reinforcing to protect occupants in the event of a major earthquake. In an effort to preserve the interior character of the building, and at the same time capitalize on an architectural opportunity, Holst externalized the new seismic bracing. Two rigid steel frames connected by steel beams accommodate fire exits, allow access to the roof garden, define an exterior patio, protect against earthquakes, and express the evolution of the structure and its place on the earth.

Water Strategies

The JVNCC incorporates a range of strategies aimed at eliminating urban runoff, protecting the overburdened Willamette River, and conserving water.

A vegetated roof provides the first round of protection; plants and soil absorb and hold rainwater for evaporation. The water that is not absorbed by the roof is channeled to an on-site bioswale. The bioswale holds and treats the water, allowing gradual percolation back into the earth. Vegetated with native plants, the green spaces use only the minimal irrigation required for plant establishment. Inside the building, low-flow plumbing fixtures support additional conservation.

Fire Strategies

Treatment of defining characteristics is a common challenge in retrofitting historic buildings. For example, existing fenestration patterns must often be preserved as part of the building's historical integrity. In the case of the JVNCC, the shell, originally designed to house materials, did not have the transparency desirable in a modern office building, and the architects were unable to open the perimeter further to light and air. As a result, the JVNCC is not optimally daylit; however, lowering the ambient lighting levels to 60 percent of typical office buildings, in combination with a daylit central atrium equipped with photo-sensors and energy-efficient glazing, did contribute to greater operational efficiency.

The Ecotrust's restored brick facade.
Photo: Dan Tyrpak

(Bottom) Renovated interior of building.
Photo: Dan Tyrpak

THE BREWERY BLOCKS
Pearl District, Portland, Oregon
GBD Architects and Gerding/Edlen Development

General Description
The largest single tract of land in the Pearl District, and Oregon's largest private development, the Brewery Blocks, which is adjacent to downtown Portland, forms a critical link between neighborhoods. It is a five-block development composed of both historic and new construction. GBD Architects and Gerding/Edlen Development Company are transforming the former Blitz Brewery into 1 million square feet of condominiums mixed with retail and office space, along with underground parking.

The sheer size of this development is both a risk and an asset. The economics of supporting such a large venture is complicated, and the success of the retail components is a significant factor in the success of the project. That said, the project's scale allows the implementation of sustainable strategies on an equally grand scale, multiplying the potential benefits through shared use and coordination among buildings. This large-scale incorporation of sustainable strategies is noteworthy, particularly with respect to fire and air. All of the buildings have applied for awards under the LEED rating system.

Fire Strategies
The Brewery Blocks uses its size and height to capitalize on the availability of the sun for light, heat, and energy, with 380 building-integrated photovoltaic panels contributing an estimated 12,000 kWh annually. In addition,

(Opposite) The exterior is a dramatic juxtaposition of the historic warehouse with the new steel bracing. Photo: Dan Tyrpak

Map of five blocks.

(Bottom) Model of five blocks. Photo: GBD Architects

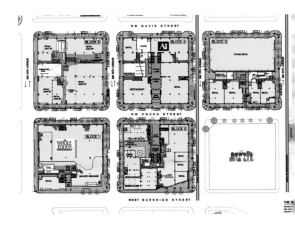

Whole Foods building. Photo: Bruce Forester

54 solar panels supply the condominium tower with hot water. High-efficiency windows equipped with light shelves help distribute daylight while preventing excessive heat gain in interior spaces. Dimmers and occupant sensors save energy and reduce glare between perimeter and interior office conditions.

Air Strategies
The first phase of construction, Block 1, included the building of a large, central, chilled water plant intended to serve the entire multi-block development. Concentrating much of the cooling equipment for the five blocks in one place freed up valuable roof area on the remaining buildings. The roofs could then be used for green space (vegetated roof and eco-roof systems) and for the installation of photovoltaic panels.

(Left) New housing within the historic district. Photo: Bruce Forester

(Right) Whole Foods building integrates a new office addition above the two-story historic structure. Photo: Bruce Forester

WIEDEN + KENNEDY BUILDING
Pearl District, Portland, Oregon
Allied Works Architecture

General Description

Wieden + Kennedy, an international advertising agency, had outgrown its headquarters in downtown Portland. As a creative enterprise, in which interaction and surroundings spark inspiration, the agency desired a space that would instill a greater sense of connection among its employees and with the community. Wieden + Kennedy enlisted Allied Works to adapt an old warehouse and cold-storage facility to this purpose. The result is an integrated solution that accomplishes structural, spatial, environmental, and programmatic goals by the insertion of a concrete core as a highly expressive element into the center of the existing building cube. The core simultaneously provides shear strength, visual and physical connections within and between floor plates, daylight, airflow, gathering space for the agency, and performance space for the community.

Earth Strategies

In addition to the wide range of recycling strategies and earth-friendly materials used throughout the project, the engagement of the Wieden + Kennedy building with the earth is expressed by its seismic strategy. Whereas the seismic bracing for the Jean Vollum Natural Capital Center was externalized to great effect, the shear strength for the Wieden + Kennedy Building resides on the inside and generates different opportunities. Seismic stability comes from the new concrete core, which both separates and connects the floors and departments. The complex vocabulary of openings and passages through the core becomes impromptu meeting places and points of observation. The center of the core is a performance space, a place where the community enters in and where a creative exchange between interior and exterior takes place.

Fire Strategies

Prior to adaptation, the exterior of the Wieden + Kennedy Building had ample fenestration, and its perimeter had plenty of available daylight, yet with its large 200 x 200 ft. floor plates, light from the perimeter did not reach the interior. This lack of daylight made the center unfit for office space. Allied Works carved the center out of the cube, opened it to the sky, and transformed it into a lantern for the surrounding office spaces. This resulted in a much more balanced lighting condition, as office spaces enjoy daylight contributed by two sides.

Postscript

The Pearl District is one of the most successful green developments in an urban context in North America. The three projects presented here demonstrate that multiple developers working toward common goals and supported by the stewardship of an inspired city government can integrate environmental responsiveness, resource efficiency, and community and cultural values in a large multi-block urban area. The Pearl District has a strong regional character and is uniquely Portland.

This singular character is due to several factors. The scale of the area is

(Opposite) Wieden + Kennedy Building exterior. Photo: Sally Schoolmaster

Building section (top) and second-floor plan (bottom). Drawing: Allied Works

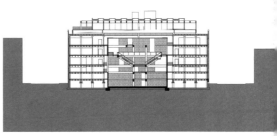

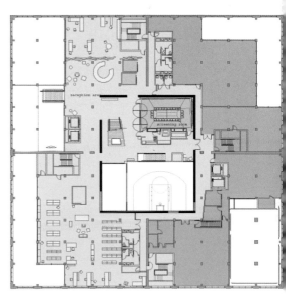

w+k
second flo

The new roof structure is composed of a double layer of glue-laminated beams. Photo: Sally Schoolmaster

pedestrian friendly, with narrow streets and a 200-foot grid block system. People walk around the neighborhood from early in the morning until late at night. The converted warehouses are unadorned brick background buildings with unusually large windows, which has allowed retrofitting for offices and housing without sacrificing natural light. The new brick and concrete-frame buildings complement the historic industrial structures. Although generally taller, they maintain the continuous street-wall character of the district. Small park spaces are woven into the neighborhood fabric, forming public areas of refuge, intimacy, and serenity. The urban cohesion of the physical environment is the Pearl's greatest strength.

While physical consistency is a strong asset, social cohesion is a problem. The Pearl District is beginning to suffer from a lack of economic and demographic diversity. It has attracted thousands of new residents of similar lifestyles and does not have the variety of family makeup, economic means, and ethnic background that makes a truly vital urban neighborhood. Industrial uses are being forced out, and the district's original "gritty" quality, an outstanding and attractive feature, has been lost. One hopes that as the final few vacant parcels are built up, the City of Portland and the federal government will partner with developers to create more low-cost housing and mixed-use projects of greater diversity.

The interactive atrium space connects all levels within the building. Photo: Sally Schoolmaster

CONCLUSION

What is the basis of architectural form? The examples in this book demonstrate that architectural form derives from the climate, site, and cultural context of the region.

The climate in the Pacific Northwest is temperate, and the resulting forms express these conditions. Where heavy snow loads are not a concern, slender roof profiles slice the sky and delicate structures meet the ground elegantly. The region is hilly, further exaggerating the relationship of a building to its site. Because temperatures are mild, roof beams can be left exposed on interior spaces, with insulation occurring on top of the beams and the roof deck. The result is richly textured interiors; a purity of architectural form remains. Large wind loads and seismic forces are expressed in structural bracing and orientation of the building on the site. The structures beautifully articulate the natural forces of the region.

What passive design strategies work in this region? The temperate climate lends itself to simple solutions that rely on natural ventilation. Smaller building forms permit operable windows and cooling towers that pull the outside air into and through these structures. Fresh air improves working conditions and connects us to the weather. In a region where the winters are long and dark, and summers are short and bright, daylighting is always a highly considered solution. Clerestory windows, skylights, and light shelves bounce light into interiors. Expressive exterior shades filter the harsh western sun but permit dappled light to permeate work spaces. Daylight keeps us attuned to the time of day and the season; filtered, it recalls the enchanting light of the surrounding forests.

The Pacific Northwest was once overgrown with immense forests, and wood is an important material. It has been historically central to the economy and remains an abundant and locally available resource. Pacific Northwest architecture is closely tied to the skill of woodcraftsmen, and forms result from this connection.

The Pacific Northwest is also a crossroads for the world. Ships, airplanes, and railroads connect us to distant areas of our continent and to the Far East. The region is an industrial hub, and steel is an available and appropriate material. The resulting architectural form takes advantage of this industry. Wooden beams meet wooden columns with custom steel connectors. Steel elevates wooden columns above the wet earth, protecting them from rot. Steel and wood allow us to design for disassembly, with the potential for easy, elegant reuse in the future. The soft, warm texture of wood highlights the crisp coldness of steel.

Design quality is at the heart of the sustainability issue. How does an architect explore the programmatic goals within a particular problem and find the best solutions? The forms, implicit in every potential building, are

(Opposite) The public thoroughfare inside Bainbridge Island City Hall. Photo: Art Grice

(Top) REI climbing wall forms a gateway into South Lake Union's sustainable development. Photo: Robert Pisano

(Bottom) REI's structure from certified wood looms over the wooded landscape of native species plants. Photo: Robert Pisano

innately responsible for the conditions of program, site, and climate. Design is the process of problem solving. It involves dialogue with many people on the design team, including architects, engineers, and client. The examples in this book represent the successful collaboration of many creative people. Sometimes the solutions are technical, requiring careful engineering and analysis and utilizing the newest mechanical systems available. Often the solutions rely on passive means for providing comfortable temperatures and lighting conditions. Every design must take into consideration the regional context, but the human context is central.

Human comfort makes for a better fit with the environment. By addressing access to daylight, good air quality, and comfortable temperatures, architects improve the human experience, and elegance in architectural form emerges. Smaller buildings allow all the occupants access to light and air. Reducing program and relying on natural phenomena reduce material and energy waste. When we focus on the relationship to the human senses, we look less at the categories and more at the phenomenology of our experience.

To quote Henry David Thoreau: "Think of our life in nature,—daily to be shown matter, to come in contact with it, Rocks, trees, wind on our cheeks! The solid earth! The actual world! The common sense! Contact! Contact! Who are we? Where are we?"

The buildings represented in this book are distinctive. They have been selected to present a range of complex and diverse approaches to sustainable design in the Pacific Northwest. They are different in scale and type but demonstrate the best creative work of architects in this region. Educating both the design team and the client is critical. By looking at existing projects, we can see what works and why. What are the best solutions for

the region? What are the creative and experimental opportunities?

How do we move forward from here? We move forward by understanding the history and unique characteristics of the region. The Pacific Northwest is steeped in innovation, connection to nature, and environmental leadership. It is the role of the architect to creatively synthesize the complex considerations of program, client, climate, site, and culture so as to build a meaningful and lasting architectural form. These forms are the new Northwest Regionalism, the environmental architecture of the Pacific Northwest.

The Merrill Addition to the University of Washington Urban Horticulture Center incorporates recycled storm water, natural ventilation, photo-voltaic panels and furniture crafted from salvaged city trees. Photo: Mary Levin

GLOSSARY

Active
A heating or cooling system that uses mechanical devices such as fans and pumps to distribute heat, or an electric lighting system.

Adaptive reuse
A process that adapts buildings for new uses while retaining their historic features. An old factory may become an apartment building, a rundown church may find new life as a restaurant, and a restaurant may become a church.

Bioswale
An open, porous landscaped channel that is graded to divert, retain, and filter site and building runoff for treatment and purification.

Black water
Used wastewater from the toilet.

Catchwater
Water collected from rain and snow for use in a building.

CDX plywood
An exterior-grade structural plywood commonly used for roof and wall sheathing.

Clerestory windows
Windows that typically are vertical and located high in a building. A means of admitting natural light into a building at a high (at or close to ceiling) level.

CMU (concrete masonry unit)
A block of hardened concrete, with or without hollow cores, designed to be laid in the same manner as brick or stone; a concrete block.

Component dimensioning
A method of design that considers the available sizes and modules of material in order to reduce waste.

Composter
A device that pulverizes and mixes decayed organic matter for use as fertilizer.

Detention pond
An impoundment, normally dry, for temporarily storing storm runoff from a drainage area and reducing the peak rate of flow.

Double-glazed skin, buffer wall
Two parallel sheets of glass with an airspace in between.

Earth-sheltering
A building that is buried in the ground, typically for the purpose of benefiting from constant subsoil temperatures and reducing the difference between inside and outside temperatures.

Ecology
The science of the interactions and relationships between living organisms and their environments.

Fly ash
A waste product of coal-fired power plants, used as a concrete admixture. It increases strength, decreases permeability, increases sulfate resistance, reduces temperature rise, reduces mixing water, and improves the pumpability and workability of concrete.

FSC (Forest Stewardship Council), FSC-certified lumber
Forest-management certification requires an inspection by an independent FSC-accredited certification body to verify that the forest complies with the international FSC Principles of Responsible Forest Management. Certified forest operations may claim that their forest products come from a responsibly managed forest. Before a certified forest operation can sell its products as FSC certified, it must also obtain chain-of-custody certification (FM/COC). Chain of custody is the path taken by raw materials from the forest to the consumer, including all successive stages of processing, transformation, manufacturing, and distribution.

GIS (geographic information system)
A system of hardware, software, and procedures designed to support the capture, management, manipulation, analysis, modeling, and display of spatially referenced data for solving complex planning and management problems.

Glare
An intense contrast in adjacent lighting conditions, often uncomfortable or painful to the eyes.

Glazed thermal buffer
See double-glazed skin, buffer wall

Gray water
Used water from all plumbing fixtures except the toilet.

Green roof
A roof with plants covering its surface for the purpose of providing a roof garden, thermal insulation, and retention of roof runoff.

Groundwater
Water that lies beneath the earth's surface.

Gypsum wallboard (GWB)
An interior facing panel consisting of a gypsum (hydrous calcium sulfate) core sandwiched between paper faces. Also called "drywall," "plaster-board."

HVAC
Heating, ventilation, and air conditioning.

Hydrolic
Related to water in all its forms.

Impermeable cap
A membrane that protects the groundwater from toxic runoff and off-gassing to the atmosphere.

Impervious paving
Paving that does not permit water to seep into it.

Infiltrate
The slow downward filtering of water through soil particles.

Infiltration pond
An infiltration pond collects stormwater and allows it to soak into the soil. This infiltration process helps recharge groundwater. Also called "retention pond."

LEED (Leadership in Energy and Environmental Design)
The LEED Green Building Rating System™ is a voluntary, consensus-based national standard for developing high-performance, sustainable buildings. Members of the U.S. Green Building Council representing all segments of the building industry developed LEED and continue to contribute to its evolution. The LEED rating system is organized into five environmental categories, and credits are earned for performance in each. Different levels of certification are awarded based on the total credits earned. The certification levels are (lowest to highest) Certified, Silver, Gold, and Platinum.

Light shelf
A horizontal reflector that divides upper and lower glazing; used to reflect light to the ceiling, even daylight distribution in a room, and reduce glare.

Living Machine™
A Living Machine is a wastewater treatment system composed of a series of tanks teeming with plants, trees, grasses, algae, koi and goldfish, tiny freshwater shrimp, snails, and a diversity of microorganisms and bacteria. Each

tank is a different mini-ecosystem designed to eat or break down waste. The process takes about four days to turn mucky water crystal clear. It is chemical free and odor free (except perhaps for the sweet fragrance of flowers).

Louver
An array of numerous sloping, closely spaced slats used to diffuse air or prevent the entry of rainwater into a ventilation opening.

Low-E glass
Glass with a low-emissivity coating. The surface coating permits the passage of most shortwave electromagnetic radiation (light and heat) but reflects most longer-wave radiation (heat).

Low-flow water fixtures
Water fixtures designed to reduce the quantity of water consumed.

MDF (medium-density fiberboard)
An engineered-wood building panel formed by breaking down softwood into wood fibers and combining it with wax and resin.

Mineral wool insulation
A highly insulating material spun from volcanic rock. Because of its high density, mineral wool is better than fiberglass at providing acoustical absorption and has a higher insulating value: R-3.7/inch for 2.5 pcf density, and R-3.9/inch for 4 pcf density. It is also a superb fire-resistive material, with a typical smoke developed rating of 0 and a flame spread rating of 0–15. Unlike fiberglass (which contains an organic binder), it can be used in direct contact with flues, stoves, and other hot objects. Mineral wool is also water repellent. Also known as "rock wool."

Native plants
Plants indigenous to a particular place or region.

OSB (oriented strand board)
A building panel composed of long shreds of wood fiber oriented in specific directions and bonded under pressure.

Passive system
A system that uses nonmechanical, nonelectrical means to satisfy heating, lighting, or cooling loads. Purely passive systems use radiation, conduction, and natural convection to distribute heat and daylight.

Photovoltaic (PV) cell
The treated semiconductor material that converts solar irradiance to electricity.

Photovoltaic system
An installation of photovoltaic modules and other components designed to produce power from sunlight and meet the power demand for a designated load.

Plenum
The space between the ceiling of a room and a structural floor above; used as a passage for ductwork, piping, and wiring.

Porous paving
Paving that permits water to percolate into the ground.

Pre-finished plywood
Plywood that is delivered to the site pre-finished with a UV lacquer and sanded to 1000 grit.

Primary-growth forest
A forest ecosystem with the principal characteristics and key elements of native ecosystems, such as complexity, structure, diversity, and an abundance of mature trees, relatively undisturbed by human activity. Human impact in such forest areas has normally been limited to low levels of hunting, fishing, and harvesting of forest products. Such ecosystems are also referred to as "mature," "old-growth," or "virgin" forests.

Rainwater harvesting
The practice of collecting, treating, and storing rain caught from a roof for use in a building.

Recycled fill
Material that would otherwise go into a landfill.

Recycled-plastic lumber
Dimensional lumber made from recycled plastic.

Regionalism
Design that reflects a region's culture, history, climate, construction practices, and materials.

Relite
A glazed opening, typically interior to a building, that borrows natural light from a nearby window or visually connects two spaces.

Remediation
Reparation, particularly having to do with damaged or toxic soil.

Retention pond
A reservoir containing a permanent pool for temporarily storing storm runoff and reducing the storm runoff rate from a drainage area.

Rock storage chamber
A solar energy storage system in which the collected heat or cold is stored in a rock bin for later use. This type of storage can be used in an active, hybrid, or even passive system.

Roof scupper
An opening in a parapet through which water drains over the edge of a flat roof.

Sand-set paving
Paving with an underbed that is separated from the structural floor deck by a layer of sand.

Secondary-growth forest
A forest that has been logged and has recovered naturally or by artificial means. Not all secondary forests contribute toward sustaining biological diversity, or goods and services, as did primary forest in the same location.

Seismic
Of, relating to, or caused by an earthquake.

Side-light
A tall, narrow window alongside a door.

Silver rating
See LEED

Solar hot-water panel
A panel that collects the sun's energy for passively heating domestic water.

Solar panel
A panel that collects the sun's energy for conversion to electricity. Also called "photovoltaic panel."

Stack effect
The cooling process of natural ventilation induced by the chimney effect, whereby a pressure differential occurs across the section of a room. Air in the room absorbs heat gained in the space, expands, loses density, and then rises to the top of the space. When it exits through high outlet openings, lower pressure is created low in the space, which draws in cooler outside air through low inlets.

Stormwater
Rainwater that enters the storm drain system and empties into lakes, rivers, streams, or the ocean.

Sunshade (external)
External shading devices can be either horizontal, vertical, or a combination of horizontal and vertical called "egg crates." These devices are overhangs that totally shade or diffuse light and heat from the sun.

Sustainable design
Design in which energy use is minimized and renewable resources are maximized; creates an enduring architecture that works within nature's systems and cycles.

Thermal bridging
The transfer of heat from one location to another, especially interior to exterior, by a conductive material.

Thermal mass
Materials with high heat capacity, such as masonry or water, used to store excess heat or coolness for later use when needed.

Trombe wall
A solar heating system consisting of a masonry thermal storage wall placed between the solar aperture and the heated space. Heat is transferred into the space by conduction through the masonry, by radiation from its inner surface, and, if vents are provided, by natural ventilation.

Urban heat island
The additional heating of air over a city that results when vegetated surfaces are replaced by asphalt, concrete, rooftops, and other man-made materials. These materials store much of the sun's energy, producing a dome of elevated air temperatures up to 10 degrees higher above a city compared to air temperatures over adjacent rural areas. Light-colored rooftops and lighter-colored pavement help dissipate heat by reflecting sunlight.

VAV (variable air volume)
A method of modulating the amount of heating or cooling effect delivered to a building by the HVAC system. The flow of air is modulated, not the temperature. VAV systems typically consist of VAV boxes that throttle supply airflow to individual zones, some mechanism to control supply-fan flow to match box demand, and the interconnecting ductwork and components.

VOC (volatile organic compounds)
Family of chemicals. The term "volatile" means that the compounds vaporize at normal room temperatures. VOCs at levels higher than the health risk limits may be harmful to the central nervous system, kidneys, or liver. VOCs may also cause irritation upon skin contact, or may irritate mucous membranes if they are inhaled. Some VOCs are known or suspected carcinogens.

Water wall-heating system
A solar heating system consisting of a thermal storage wall of water in containers placed between the solar aperture and the heated space. Heat is transferred into the space by conduction and convection through the water and by radiation from the inner wall surface to the room.

Watershed
The specific land area that drains water into a river system or other body of water.

Wetland
A general term used to describe an area that is neither fully terrestrial nor fully aquatic. Such areas range in character from the majestic cypress swamps of the southern United States to shallow, unimpressive depressions that hold water for at most only a few weeks out of the year.

PROJECT INFORMATION

CHAPTER 4. SITE: BUILDING THROUGH ECOLOGICAL PLANNING

CEDAR RIVER WATERSHED EDUCATION CENTER

19901 Cedar Falls Road S.W.
North Bend, Washington 98045

Project Team
Owner/client: Seattle Public Utilities
Architect, landscape architect: Jones & Jones
Civil, sanitary: Anne Symonds & Associates
Structural: Pai Lin Engineering
Mechanical: de Montigny Engineers
Electrical: Coffman Engineers
Public artist: Dan Corson
General contractor: Berschauer Phillips Construction

Project Statistics
Completion date: October 2001
Project size: 10,000 square feet interior, 4,000 square feet covered exterior
Site size: 4.5 acres
Program: Visitors center, meeting rooms, interpretive exhibits, research library, learning laboratory, forest court

VASHON ISLAND TRANSFER AND RECYCLING STATION

18900 Westside Highway S.W.
Vashon Island, WA 98070

Project Team
Client: King County Department of Natural Resources, Solid Waste Division
Architect: The Miller/Hull Partnership
Landscape architect: Susan Black and Associates
Civil and prime consultant: Thomas/Wright, Inc.
Sustainability consultant: Paladino Consulting
Mechanical, electrical: CH2M Hill
Structural: H. K. Kim Engineers, Inc.
Testing, geotechnical: HWA GeoSciences, Inc.
Artist: Deborah Mersky
Public relations: Triangle Associates
Contractor: Pease Construction, Inc.

Project Statistics
Completion date: April 1999
Project size: 10,000 square feet transfer building, 400 square feet scale-house
Site size: 6 acres
Program: Recycling and transfer facility

ENVIRONMENTAL SERVICES BUILDING
9850 Sixty-fourth Street W.
University Place, Washington 98467

Project Team
Client: Pierce County Public Works and Utilities
Architect: The Miller/Hull Partnership
Planning, interiors: Arai Jackson
Landscape architect: Bruce Dee and Associates
Mechanical, electrical: AE Associates
Geotechnical: GeoEngineers, Inc.
Civil: SvR Design Company
Structural: AHBL
Traffic: Transportation Engineering Northwest
Cost consulting: Roen Associates

Project Statistics
Completion date: 2002
Project size: 50,000 square feet
Site size: 930 acres
Program: Office space for Pierce County Environmental Services Division, meeting rooms, public environmental display space

MAPLE VALLEY LIBRARY
21844 S.E. 248th Street
Maple Valley, Washington 98038

Project Team
Client: King County Library System
Architects: Johnston Architects in collaboration with Cutler Anderson Architects
Mechanical, electrical: McGowan Broz Engineers, Inc.
Civil: SvR Design Company
Structural: Swenson Say Faget
Contractor: R. Miller Construction

Project Statistics
Completion date: 2000
Project size: 10,200 square feet
Site size: 2 acres
Program: Reading room, children's area, young adults area, computer carrels, study tables, circulation and reference desks, staff areas, meeting room, study room, parking for 60 vehicles

BRADNER GARDEN COMMUNITY BUILDING

1730 Bradner Place S.
Seattle, Washington 98144

Project Team
Clients: City of Seattle Department of Parks and Recreation, Friends of
Bradner Garden
Architect: Scot Carr, SHED
Structural: Perbix/Bydonen
Contractor: Norse Construction, Inc.

Project Statistics
Completion date: 2003
Project size: 1,700 square feet roof area, 1,000 square feet enclosed
space
Site size: 1.5 acres
Program: Meeting room, tool room, utility room, restroom

MATERIALS TESTING FACILITY

900 E. Kent Avenue
Vancouver, British Columbia V5X 2X9

Project Team
Client: City of Vancouver
Architect: Busby + Associates Architects
Landscape architect: City of Vancouver staff
Project manager: David Desrochers, P. Eng., City of Vancouver
Structural: Fast & Epp Partners
Mechanical: Keen Engineering Company, Ltd.
Electrical: Reid Crowther & Partners, Ltd.
Construction manager: Ken King & Associates

Project Statistics
Completion date: 1999
Project size: 4,280 square feet
Site size: 2.2 acres
Program: Offices, meeting rooms, laboratories

PETITE MAISON DE WEEKEND REVISITED

Wexner Center for the Arts
Columbus, Ohio

Project Team
Client: Wexner Center for the Arts
Architect: Patkau Architects
Structural: Fast + Epp Partners
Contractor: Patkau Architects

Project Statistics
Completion date: 1998
Project size: 200 square feet
Program: Sitting/sleeping space, toilet room

CHAPTER 6. LIGHT AND VENTILATION: CLIMATE-RESPONSIVE ENCLOSURE

ISLANDWOOD
4450 Blakely Avenue N.E.
Bainbridge Island, Washington 98110

Project Team
Clients: Puget Sound Environmental Learning Center and Debbi Brainerd,
President and Founder
Architect: Mithun Architects + Designers + Planners
Landscape architect: Berger Partnership
Master planning: Bill Isley
Civil: Browne Engineering
Structural: Skilling Ward Magnusson Barkshire
Mechanical: Keen Engineering Company, Ltd.
Electrical: Cross Engineers, Inc.
Accessibility: Studio Pacifica
Water, septic alt.: 2020 Engineering
Acoustics: Michael R. Yantis
Kitchen design: Clevenger Associates
Green reviewer: Archemy Consulting
General contractors: RAFN Construction, Drury Construction, Doug
Woodside

Project Statistics
Completion date: Spring 2002
Project size: 70,574 square feet
Site size: 255 acres
Program: Interpretive center, learning studios, dining area with kitchen,
administrative offices, arts studios, maintenance building, guest housing,
staff housing, interpretive trails

PIER 56
1201 Alaskan Way
Seattle, Washington 98101

Project Team
Client, owner, developer: Martin Smith, Inc.
Architect: Mithun Architects + Designers + Planners
Structural: Coughlin Porter Lundeen
Mechanical: Holaday Parks
Electrical: Cross Engineers, Inc.
HVAC: Keen Engineering Company, Ltd.
Acoustics: Michael R. Yantis
Contractor: Edifice Construction

Completion date: 2000
Project size: 27,340 square feet
Site size: 27,340 square feet
Program: Renovation of existing historic structure to house Mithun offices

TELUS/WILLIAM FARRELL BUILDING REVITALIZATION

Robson Street
Vancouver, British Columbia V6B 3K9

Project Team
Client: Telus Communication Services
Architect: Busby + Associates Architects
Structural: Read Jones Christoffersen
Mechanical: Keen Engineering Company, Ltd.
Electrical: Reid Crowther & Partners, Ltd.
General contractor: Dominion Construction Company

Project Statistics
Completion date: 2001
Project size: 130,000 square feet
Site size: 60,000 square feet
Program: Offices, retail/commercial, presentation space

CHAPTER 7. TECHNOLOGY AND MATERIALS: THE INTEGRATED FUTURE

SEATTLE JUSTICE CENTER AND SEATTLE CIVIC CENTER PLAN

600 Fifth Avenue
Seattle, Washington 98124

Project Team
Client: City of Seattle
Architect: NBBJ Architects
Landscape architect: Gustafson Partners, Ltd.
Civil: SvR Design Company
Structural: Skilling Ward Magnusson Barkshire
Mechanical: CDI Engineers
Electrical: Abacus
Consulting engineer: Ove Arup and Partners
General contractor: Hoffman Construction Company

Project Statistics
Completion date: August 2002
Project size: 310,500 square feet
Site size: 80,000 square feet
Program: Open and enclosed offices, spaces associated with police head-
quarters and city courts

BAINBRIDGE ISLAND CITY HALL

280 Madison Avenue N.
Bainbridge Island, Washington 98110

Project Team
Client: City of Bainbridge Island
Architect: The Miller/Hull Partnership
Planner, landscape architect: Cascade Design Collaborative
Civil: SvR Design Company
Structural: KPFF Consulting Engineers
Mechanical: The Greenbusch Group
Geotechnical: Myers Biodynamics
Electrical: Sparling
Environmental consultant: O'Brien & Company
Contractor: Columbia Pacific Contractors, Inc.
Construction manager: Elmquist Associates

Project Statistics
Completion date: February 2000
Project size: 24,500 square feet
Site size: 2.5 acres
Program: Administrative offices, mayor's office, community resource and information center, council meeting room

JEAN VOLLUM NATURAL CAPITAL CENTER (ECOTRUST)

Pearl District, 721 N.W. Ninth Avenue
Portland, Oregon 97209

Project Team
Client: Ecotrust
Architect: Holst Architecture
Landscape architect: Nevue Ngan Associates
Structural: KPFF Consulting Engineers
Mechanical, electrical, plumbing: Interface Engineering, Inc.
Contractor: Walsh Construction Company

Project Statistics
Completion date: 2001
Project size: 70,000 square feet
Site size: 90,000 square feet
Program: Offices, retail

THE BREWERY BLOCKS

Pearl District, bounded by W. Burnside Street, N.W. Davis Street,
N.W. Fourteenth Avenue, and N.W. Tenth Avenue
Portland, Oregon 97209

Project Team
Client: Gerding/Edlen Development Company
Architect: GBD Architects
Structural: KPFF Consulting Engineers

Mechanical, electrical, plumbing: Glumac International
Environmental building consultant: River City Resource Group
Commissioning agent: Glumac International
Energy analysis: Solarc Architecture
Contractor: Hoffman Construction, R & H Construction

Project Statistics
Completion date: 2004
Project size: 1.7 million square feet
Site size: 5 city blocks
Program: Condominiums, offices, retail, parking

WIEDEN + KENNEDY BUILDING
Pearl District, 224 N.W. Thirteenth Avenue
Portland, Oregon 97209

Project Team
Clients: Wieden + Kennedy, Gerding/Edlen Development Corporation
Architect: Allied Works Architecture
Structural, civil: KPFF Consulting Engineers
Mechanical: Manfull-Curtis, Glumac International
Electrical: James D. Graham
Lighting: Horton Lees
Acoustics, audiovisuals: Ove Arup and Partners
Theater: Theatre Projects
Color: Donald Kaufman Color
Contractor: R & H Construction

Project Statistics
Completion date: October 1999
Project size: 200,000 square feet
Site size: 90,000 square feet
Program: Offices, retail, art gallery, performance space

NOTES AND REFERENCES

PREFACE AND ACKNOWLEDGMENTS

1. Christian Norberg-Schulz, *Principles of Modern Architecture* (London: Andreas Papadakis Publisher, 2000), p. 89.

INTRODUCTION

1. Harwell Hamilton Harris, "A Collection of His Writings and Buildings," *Student Publication of the School of Design North Carolina State of the University of North Carolina at Raleigh,* vol. 14, no. 5 (1965), p. 29.

CHAPTER 1

1. David Buerge, "Visionaries," in *Washingtonians, A Biographical Portrait of the State,* ed. David Brewster and David Buerge (Seattle: Sasquatch Books, 1988), p. 159.
2. Joel Garreau, *The Nine Nations of North America* (Boston: Houghton Mifflin, 1981).
3. Arthur R. Kruckeberg, *The Natural History of Puget Sound Country* (Seattle: University of Washington Press, 1991), p. 39.
4. Arthur Erickson, *The Architecture of Arthur Erickson* (New York: Harper and Row, 1988), p. 21.
5. Quoted in Lisa C. Kennan-Meyer, "Gene Zema: Northwest Architect," M.Arch. thesis, University of Washington, 1987, p. 7.

CHAPTER 2

1. Douglas S. Kelbaugh, dean of the College of Architecture and Urban Planning, University of Michigan, remarks in a personal conversation on the Three "E's" of sustainability, June 2004.
2. Hilary Stewart, *Cedar* (Seattle: University of Washington Press; Vancouver: Douglas and McIntyre, 1984), p. 19.
3. Quoted in Thomas Veith, "A Northwest Architecture," *Column 5: University of Washington Journal of Architecture* (1991), p. 31.
4. Grant Hildebrand, "Elsworth Storey," in *Shaping Seattle Architecture: A Historical Guide to the Architects,* ed. Jeffrey Karl Ochsner (Seattle: University of Washington Press in association with the American Institute of Architects Seattle Chapter and the Seattle Architectural Foundation, 1994), p. 104.
5. Colin Porteous, *The New Eco-Architecture: Alternatives from the Modern Movement* (London: Spon Press, 2002), p. 58.
6. Meredith L. Clausen, *Pietro Belluschi: Modern American Architect* (Cam-

bridge, Mass.: MIT Press, 1994), p. 91.

7. Teiji Itoh, *The Elegant Japanese House: Traditional Sukiya Architecture* (New York: John Weatherhill, 1969), p. 158.

8. David A. Rash, "Paul Hayden Kirk," in *Shaping Seattle Architecture,* p. 252.

9. Sally Woodbridge, "The Great Northwest Revival," *Progressive Architecture* (July 1974), p. 57.

10. Douglas Kelbaugh, *Common Place: Toward Neighborhood and Regional Design* (Seattle: University of Washington Press, 1997), pp. 51–86.

CHAPTER 3

1. G. Z. Brown and Mark DeKay, *Sun, Wind, and Light: Architectural Design Strategies* (New York: John Wiley & Sons, 2001), p. xiv.

2. Arthur R. Kruckeberg, *The Natural History of Puget Sound Country* (Seattle: University of Washington Press, 1991), p. 437.

3. Quoted in Eoin Cofaigh, John Olley, and Owen Lewis, *The Climatic Dwelling* (London: James and James, 1996), p. 20.

4. Edward Mazria, *Passive Solar Energy Book* (Emmaus, Penn.: Rodale Press, 1979), pp. 406–28.

5. For a series of diagrams illustrating these principles, see Brown and DeKay, *Sun, Wind, and Light,* pp. 146–50.

6. Mithun Architects + Designers + Planners, *Resource Guide for Sustainable Development in an Urban Environment* (City of Seattle), p.152.

GLOSSARY REFERENCES

"About FSC Certification," in *Forest Stewardship Council* (Bonn: Forest Stewardship Council, International Center, 2003). Cited 8 August 2004, available at http://www.fsc.org/fsc/about/about_fsc/certification.

Edward Allen, *Fundamentals of Building Construction Materials and Methods* (New York: John Wiley and Sons, 1999).

G. Z. Brown and Mark DeKay, *Sun, Wind, and Light: Architectural Design Strategies* (New York: John Wiley and Sons, 2001).

"Definition," *Battery Park City.* Cited 8 August 2004, available at http://www.batteryparkcity.org/green_glossary_v4.htm.

Scott Freundschuh, "Q2.1: What in the world is a 'GIS'?" *The Geographic Information Systems FAQ* (Washington, D.C.: U.S. Census Bureau, 2001). Cited 8 August 2004, available at http://www.census.gov/cgi-bin/geo/gisfaq?Q2.1.

Glossary, *Photovoltaic Systems Research and Development* (Sandia National Laboratories, 2002). Cited 8 August 2004, available at http://www.sandia.gov/pv/docs/glossary.htm#AnchorP-R.

Glossary, *You Think!* (The World Bank Group, 2004). Cited 8 August 2004, available at http://youthink.worldbank.org/glossary.php#w.

"Glossary of Stormwater Terms," *Stormwater Management Division* (Los Angeles: 2004). Cited 8 August 2004, available at http://www.lastormwater.org/Pages/glossary.htm.

"Insulation Alternatives: Non-Fiberglass Batts," *Tool Base Services* (Upper Marlboro, Md.: NAHB Research Center, 2004). Cited 8 August 2004, available at http://www.toolbase.org/tertiaryT.asp?DocumentID=3930&CategoryID=140.

Leadership in Energy and Environmental Design (U.S. Green Building Council, 2003). Cited 8 August 2004, available at http://www.usgbc.org/leed/leed_main.asp.

Baker H. Morrow, *A Dictionary of Landscape Architecture* (Albuquerque: University of New Mexico Press, 1988).

David A. Perry, *Forest Ecosystems* (Baltimore: The Johns Hopkins University Press, 1994).

"Primary (Woodland) Forest," *Proceedings: Second Expert Meeting on Harmonizing Forest-Related Definitions for Use by Various Stakeholders* (Rome: Food and Agriculture Organization of the United Nations, 2002). Cited 8 August 2004, available at http://www.fao.org/DOCREP/005/Y4171E/Y4171E36.htm.

"Secondary (Woodland) Forest," *Proceedings: Second Expert Meeting on Harmonizing Forest-Related Definitions for Use by Various Stakeholders* (Rome: Food and Agriculture Organization of the United Nations, 2002). Cited 8 August 2004, available at http://www.fao.org/DOCREP/005/Y4171E/Y4171E36.htm.

"Stormwater Facilities," *Natural Resources and Parks* (King County, 2003). Cited 8 August 2004, available at http://dnr.metrokc.gov/wlr/dss/rd-ponds.htm.

Steven Strom and Kurt Nathan, *Site Engineering for Landscape Architects* (New York: Van Nostrand Reinhold, 1993).

"VOC's," *Environmental Issues* (About Inc.). Cited 8 August 2004, available at http://environment.about.com/cs/glossary/g/voc.htm.

"Wetlands Definition." Cited 8 August 2004, available at http://agen521.www.ecn.purdue.edu/AGEN521/epadir/wetlands/definition.html.

"What Are the Health Risks Associated with VOC Contamination?" *Minnesota Department of Health* (2004). Cited 8 August 2004, available at http://www.health.state.mn.us/divs/eh/hazardous/vocs.html#what3.

"What Is Adaptive Reuse?" *Architecture Glossary* (About Inc.). Cited 8 August 2004, available at http://architecture.about.com/library/blgloss-reuse.htm.

Jeff Wolovitz, "The Living Machine," *Penn State/Research* 21, no. 3 (September 2000). Cited 8 August 2004, available at http://www.rps.psu.edu/0009/machine.html.

INDEX

Aalto, Alvar, 32, 41
Albertson, A. H., 15
Allied Works Architecture, 123, 145
American Institute of Architects, 7, 23
American Southwest, xi, 31
Anderson, Guy, 5
Anderson Corporation, 27
Arai Jackson, 73
Arts and Crafts period, 11, 12, 15, 16, 17

Bainbridge Island City Hall, 123, 131, 134
Banham, Reyner, 123
Barnett, Dianna Lopez, 103
Bassetti, Fred, 23
Bay Area School, 16
Beaux-Arts, 17
Belluschi, Pietro, 5, 7, 17, 19, 20, 21, 22
Berger Partnership, 105
Berwick, Robert A. D., 17, 21
Binning, B. C., 21
bioswale, 40, 49, 61, 76, 139
Boeing Airplane Company, 4
BOORA Architects, 46, 47
Bosworth, Thomas, 30
Bradner Garden, 87
Bradner Garden Community Building, 45, 85
Brainerd, Paul and Debbi, 105
Brewery Blocks, 123, 141
Brown, G.Z., 35
Buerge, David, 4
Bumgardner Partnership, 30
Busby + Associates Architects, 93, 117
Busby, Peter, xii

California Stick Style, 19
Carr, Scot, xii, 87, 88
Cascadia, 3
Cedar River Watershed, 55
Cedar River Watershed Education Center, 55, 63, 65
Central Precinct Police Station, 45
Civic Center Plan, Seattle, 125, 127
Clackamas High School, 46, 47

Clausen, Meredith, 21
Cloepfil, Brad, xii
Coastal Temperate Rain Forest Zone, 3
Coast Salish, 11, 13
Columbia River Valley, 3, 4
Congrès Internationaux d'Architecture Moderne (CIAM), 7, 23
Cornell University, 19
Critical Regionalism, 33
Cutler Anderson Architects, 35, 79
Cutler, James, xii, 33, 80, 82
Culter Residence, 28
Cutter, Kirtland, 15, 16

DeKay, Mark, 35
Departmental of Architecture, University of Washington, xii, 23
Doyle, Albert, 20
Duwamish River, 3
Dymaxion House, 17

earth-sheltered design, 36
Ecotopia, 4
Ecotrust building, 137
Environmental Services Building, Pierce County, Washington, xviii, 73
Eppich Residence, 29
Equitable Building, 22
Erickson, Arthur, 5, 28

Faculty Club, University of Washington, 27
Fernandez-Galiano, Luis, 85
Fisher Pavilion, 38
Flanders Lofts, 50
Forest Park, Portland, Oregon, 20
Fountainebleau, American School of Paris, 19
Frampton, Kenneth, xv
Fraser River Valley, 3
FSC-certified lumber, 88
Fuller, Buckminster, 17

Garreau, Joel, 4
Gastown, Vancouver, B.C., 31
Gasworks Park, 39

Gay, Henry, 5
GBD Architects, 123, 141
Gearhart, Oregon, 20
Gerding/Edlen Development, 123, 141
Goldberg, David, xii
Gordon Smith Residence, 28, 29
Gould, Carl, 15, 17
Grand Coulee Dam, 4
Green River, 3
green roof, 61
Greenwood Residence, 43
Gropius, Walter, 17
Group Health Cooperative Clinic, 26
Gustafson Guthrie Nichols, Ltd. (GGN), 125, 127

Haag, Richard, 39
Haida, 6
Hansen Residence, 37
Harris, Harwell Hamilton, xv
Health House, 17
Helliwell + Smith, 43
Henry, Alix, vii, xii, 44, 48, 91
Heritage Courtyard, 65
Hildbrand, Grant, 16
Hollingsworth, Fred, 7, 28
Holmes, Lister, 17
Holst Architecture, 123, 138
Hull, Robert, xii

International Style, xv, 11, 18, 19, 22, 26
IslandWood, 47, 103, 105, 108, 109
Itoh, Teiji, 25

Jean Vollum Natural Capital Center (JVNCC), 137, 138, 139, 145
Johnston Architects, 79
Johnston, Ray, 82
Jones & Jones Architects and Landscape Architects, Ltd., 55, 56, 58, 63

Kelbaugh, Douglas, 33
Kerr House, 20
Kerry House, 19
Kimmick Residence, 32
King County Arts Commission, 67
Kirk, Paul Hayden, 7, 23, 25, 27, 47
Kruckeberg, Arthur, 39

Lawrence B. Culter Residence, 28
Lawrence, Jacob, 5
Lea House, 28
Le Corbusier, 7, 17, 18, 19, 99

LEED™ (rating), 129, 141
Lillis Business Complex, 45
longhouse, 6
Lopez Island, 28, 35, 38
Lovett, Wandell, 7
low-Voc coating, 88

Malaysia, xi
Maple Valley Library, 33, 79
Maple Valley, Washington, 79, 82
Massey, Geoffrey, 28
Materials Testing Facility, 85, 93
Maybeck, Bernard, 1, 16
McHarg, Ian, 53
Mercy Residence, 37
Merrill Hall, University of Washington, 151
Miller/Hull Partnership, xii, 32, 38, 40, 44, 46, 67, 69, 70, 73, 74, 75, 123, 131, 134
Mithun Architects + Designers + Planners, 47, 48, 103, 105, 106, 111, 112
Modernism, xi, 7, 18, 30; regional, 11
Mount Angel Library, 32
Murase, Robert, 40, 49

Native American, xi, 6, 7, 11
native landscape, 57
natural ventilation, 46, 73, 95, 96, 108, 113, 115, 117, 120, 149
NBBJ, 123, 125, 126, 127, 129
Neutra, Richard, 17
Newton Library, 50
Norberg-Schulz, Christian, xi, 20, 51
Northwest "Contemporary" Style, 5, 30
Northwest Energy Alliance–Lighting Design Lab, 45
Northwest Modern Movement, xii
Northwest Regionalism, xv, xvi, xvii, 3, 5
Northwest Regional Style, xvii, 7, 8, 23
Northwest School, 7, 23
NW Federal Credit Union, 44

O'Brien & Company, 131
Olmsted, Susan, vii, xii
Olson, Paul, xii
Olson, Sim, 38
Oregon Museum of Science and Industry, 49
Ove Arup and Partners, 126, 129

Pacific Ocean, 5
passive solar strategies, 41, 44, 64
Patkau Architects, 50
Patkau, John, xii

Pearl District, Portland, Oregon, 123, 137, 138, 141, 145, 146
Petite Masion de Weekend, 85, 99
photovoltaic cells, 45
photovoltaic panels, 88, 99, 105, 107
Pier 56, 111
Pierce County, Washington, 73
Pike Place Market, 31
Pilchuck Glass School, 30
Pioneer Square, 31
Porteous, Colin, 17, 18
Prakash, Vikram, ii, xii
Pratt, C. E., 7, 17, 21
Prices, Lionel, 17, 23, 28, 32
pueblos, xi
Puget Sound, 5, 13, 22, 106, 115
Puget Sound Air Pollution Control Agency, 46
Putnam Residence, 27

raised floor, 75, 119
Rash, David, 27
Rattlesnake Lake, 55, 56, 57, 61
Raymond, Antonin, 19
recycled construction waste, 70
recycled materials, 68, 74, 94, 132, 138
Reeve House, 35
regional character, xi
regional style, xi
REI, 150
Rhone & Iredale, 32
Richard Lea House, 28
Roberts, Sian, xii
Roquebrune-Cap-Martin, France, 99
Rottle, Nancy, xii

Salish, 6
Sea Ranch, 30
Seattle Golf and Country Club, 16
Seattle Justice Center, 123, 125, 126, 127, 128, 129
Seattle Sculpture Park, 39
Sedgewick Library, 32
SERA Architects, 36, 40, 45
SHED, 87
Skagit River Valley, 3
Skidmore, Owings and Merrill, 51
Smith Residence, 28, 29
Sokol Blosser Winery, 36
solar index, 42
South Lake Union, 137, 150
SRG Partnership, 45
Steinbrueck, Victor, 7, 23, 27
Stewart, Hilary, 13

Storey, Elsworth, 12, 15
stormwater, management, 76
Strait of Georgia, 5
Strait of Jaun de Fuca, 5
Stuart, Kirk and Durham, 26
Stuhr, Jeff, xii
Stuttgart, Germany, 17
sustainable design, xi, 11, 12
Sutor House, 20

Telus building, 117, 119, 120
Telus/William Farrell building, 117, 119, 120
Terry, Roland, 7, 23, 28, 32, 38
Thiry, Paul, 5, 17, 18
Thomas/Wright, Inc., 67
Thoreau, Henry David, 150
Thorton, Peter, 17
Tulalip Bay Community Center, 30

University of British Columbia, 32
U.S. Department of Energy, 42

Vallaster and Corl, 50
Vancouver, B.C., xii, 5, 17
Vancouver School, 28
van der Rohe, Mies, 17
Vashon Island, 67
Vashon Island Transfer and Recycling Station, 67, 68
vernacular, Northwest Coast Native, 6
Vine Street, 49
Vollum Natural Capital Center (JVNCC), 137, 138, 139, 145

Wakasham, 13
Water Pollution Control Laboratory, 40, 45, 48, 49
Watzek House, 20
Weinstein/Copeland, 45
Weiss/Manfredi, 39
Weyerhaeuser Company, 27
Weyerhaeuser Headquarters Building, 51
Whole Foods building, 142, 143
Wieden + Kennedy Building, 123, 145
Willamette River, 3, 45
Wilsonville City Hall, 46
Wolf, Scott, xii
Woodbridge, Sally, 30
Wood Research House, 27
Wright, Frank Lloyd, 21

Yeon, John, 7, 17, 19, 21

Zema, Gene, 23